100 Reproducible Reading Formative Assessments:

Standards-Based Assessments Designed to Increase Student Achievement

By Tanja S. Brannen, Ed. D.

ASSESSMENTS:

- MAIN IDEA
- SUPPORTING DETAILS
- INFERENCES
- CAUSE AND EFFECT
- COMPARE AND CONTRAST
- CHRONOLOGICAL ORDER
- AUTHOR'S PURPOSE AND PERSPECTIVE
- WORD ANALYSIS
- CONTEXT CLUES
- SYNONYMS/ANTONYMS

● **Great for the Differentiated Classroom**

● **Helps Pinpoint Areas of Skill Strengths and Weaknesses**

● **Non-Fictional and Fictional Passages**

Grades 4 - 8

A TO Z™

BRANE
Educational
Consultants
www.braneconsulting.com

A Common Sense Approach to Effective Reading Instruction

ABOUT THE AUTHOR

Tanja S. Brannen draws on many years of teaching in the classroom, best practice teaching strategies, and educational research to develop quality educational products with student achievement in mind.

Cover and graphic design by Byrd Graphics, Inc., Rochester, NY 14612

Copyright ©2011 by Tanja S. Brannen

Published by BRANE Educational Consultants, Inc.

Inquiries may be addressed to:
BRANE Publishing Co. | 3555 Raney Road | Titusville, FL 32780

Printed in the United States of America

ISBN 978-0-9828338-1-0

100 Reproducible Reading Formative Assessments:

Standards-Based Assessments Designed to Increase Student Achievement

By Tanja S. Brannen, Ed. D.

Great for the Differentiated Classroom

**Helps Pinpoint Areas
of Skill Strengths
and Weaknesses**

Non-Fictional and Fictional Passages

CONTENTS

CONTENTS

INTRODUCTION

Formative reading assessments can be the difference between success and failure for students. Teachers who have successful track records in teaching reading often point to formative reading assessments as being the key to their students' successes.

Why are formative reading assessments so valuable? Formative assessments allow teachers to reflect on what has been taught, what has been learned, and whether to move forward with instruction or reteach the lessons.

Formative reading assessments can answer the following questions: Have the students mastered the reading skill? Should the reading skill be retaught? What are the students' weakest reading skills? What are the students' strongest reading skills? Who needs to have the reading skill retaught?

This book is designed so that classroom teachers can quickly ascertain whether or not the students within the class are ready to begin a new reading skill or if they need to continue practicing a reading skill they have not mastered.

Ten story sets are included in this book. Each story set is composed of a story and 10 formative assessments that include the following: main idea, supporting details, inferences, cause and effect, comparison and contrast, chronological order, author's purpose and perspective, word analysis, context clues, and synonyms and antonyms.

100 FORMATIVE ASSESSMENTS are contained within this book!

Formative Assessments Should Be
BLISS!™

Administrators and teachers often visualize the formative assessment process as being a grading-intensive, in-depth event. A good formative assessment is the tool a teacher can use to determine who understands the concept, to what degree they understand the concept, and who does not understand the concept at all. Formative assessments should not create MISERY! In fact, the formative assessment process can and should be pure BLISS™ for the teacher and the student. What do I mean by BLISS?™ BLISS™ is an acronym that represents my five components for effective formative assessments. BLISS™ formative assessments are Brief, Legitimate, Immediate, Supportive, and Simple.

Brief:
Formative assessments should be three or four questions linked to a specific skill or concept just taught.

Legitimate:
The formative assessment should test what was taught.

Immediate:
The teacher walks and checks for correct responses—immediately. The teacher can determine the percentage of students who understand the skill or concept. The teacher then has to decide to reteach the concept, expand the instruction, or teach a new concept.

Supportive:
The teacher focuses on student needs for upcoming instruction. Results from the formative assessment are used as the Realignment Point for the teacher's instruction. The Realignment Point is simply the point at which the teacher examines the content the students have mastered after instruction and realigns the instruction to meet the students' new instructional needs.

Simple:
A quick and easy measure of whether the students got it or not.

Author's Note: The Realignment Point is a term coined by the author to describe the point of instruction at which the teacher must decide whether to move forward with instruction or reteach the lesson or portions of the lesson.

Why the Ocean is Salty
A FILIPINO FOLKTALE

Long ago there lived a giant by the name of Angelo. Angelo was the only son of the king of the giants. Angelo was a hard worker and he loved to wander the land and help other people. When Angelo was not helping other people, he enjoyed wandering in the mountains and digging many deep caves.

One bright sunny day, Angelo walked down from the mountains to the seashore. Now at this time the waters of the ocean were pure and fresh. People and animals could drink the waters of the ocean because there was no salt in the water.

As Angelo was walking along the beach, he saw a woman crying. The crying woman was Freda. Freda explained that she lived in one of the deep, dark caves he had dug. She told Angelo that she was tired of living in the subterranean cave. Freda begged Angelo to build a large house beside the ocean for her. Freda thought she would be happy living in a big house by the ocean.

Angelo felt sorry for Freda and promised her he would do as she asked. Freda said the house must be large and it must be built of bricks as white as snow.

Soon Angelo began his task. Angelo could not find any bricks as white as snow. The only thing he could find that was pure white was salt. Angelo had never seen salt before and he thought it was beautiful. Angelo spent many months cutting huge bricks of white salt and using the bricks to build the house.

When the house was finished Freda began to cry again because she thought the white salt house next to the ocean was not large enough for her. She cried for days. As Freda cried, her tears began to dissolve the salt and wash the house away. Freda's tears eventually washed all of her house into the ocean. The ocean water became salty due to Freda's tears. Freda demanded that Angelo build her another house. Angelo said if Freda wanted a new house, then she would have to build it. Freda then cried all the way back to her cave.

FORMATIVE ASSESSMENT:
Main Idea

1 What would be another good title for this story?

    A. The Gentle Woman

    B. How the Weeping Woman Made the Sea Salty

    C. The Cruel Giant

    D. all of the above

2 The main idea of the passage

    A. is to tell a folktale of how the ocean became salty.

    B. is to describe how to use salt in building a sturdy home.

    C. is to praise Angelo for being a great builder.

    D. is to praise Freda for being kind to other people.

3 The central point of the first paragraph is

    A. to introduce the reader to the character of Angelo.

    B. to explain to the reader how the ocean became salty.

    C. to explain who dug caves in the mountains.

    D. to introduce the reader to the character of Freda.

FORMATIVE ASSESSMENT:
Supporting Details

(1) Which statement is best supported by information in the story?

    A. Freda hates to cry.

    B. Angelo dislikes hearing people weep.

    C. Freda is generous.

    D. Freda is greedy.

(2) Before the salt mansion dissolved, the ocean was

    A. wild and untamed.

    B. calm and peaceful.

    C. pure and clean.

    D. fresh and salty.

(3) Which sentence best supports why Angelo helped Freda?

    A. Freda explained that she lived in one of the deep caves he had dug.

    B. Angelo felt sorry for Freda and promised her he would do as she asked.

    C. When the house was finished Freda began to cry again because she thought the white salt house next to the ocean was not large enough for her.

    D. Angelo was tired of hearing Freda cry.

(4) Why was Freda crying at the end of the story?

    A. Freda had to return to the cave to live.

    B. Angelo was tired of hearing Freda cry.

    C. She thought the white salt home next to the ocean was not large enough for her.

    D. Freda was so happy to be living in a big house by the ocean.

FORMATIVE ASSESSMENT:
Inferences

(1) The author might agree

   A. Angelo should make the woman a new, larger mansion.

   B. Angelo's work was poor.

   C. Freda was ungrateful.

   D. the water in the ocean tasted better after the salt dissolved.

(2) The reader can infer that

   A. salt is not a good building material.

   B. it is not good to build salt houses too close to the ocean.

   C. some people are not grateful when someone does a favor for them.

   D. all of the answers are correct.

(3) The reader can conclude that

   A. Angelo was a selfish man.

   B. Freda had a good sense of humor.

   C. Angelo was kind.

   D. Freda had a cheery personality.

(4) Based on the information in the story, what do you think Freda would never do?

   A. Return to the cave to live.

   B. Build her own home.

   C. Ask another person to build her a house.

   D. Ask Angelo for a third time to build her another house.

FORMATIVE ASSESSMENT:
Cause and Effect

(1) At the beginning of the story, why was the woman crying?

    A. The woman was lost.

    B. The woman was tired of living in a cave.

    C. Angelo refused to build the woman a house.

    D. The woman's house was made of salt.

(2) Why did Angelo agree to build a house for the woman?

    A. Freda was crying and Angelo felt sorry for her.

    B. Freda said she would pay Angelo.

    C. Angelo had never worked with salt before.

    D. Freda was tired of digging caves.

(3) Why did Freda cry after the house was built?

    A. The house was the wrong color.

    B. The house was not large enough.

    C. The house was unattractive.

    D. The house should have been built on the mountaintop.

(4) According to the story, why did the ocean become salty?

    A. Angelo threw blocks of salt into the ocean.

    B. Salt deposits were in the ocean.

    C. The rain washed salt into the ocean.

    D. Freda's tears washed the salt house into the ocean.

FORMATIVE ASSESSMENT:
Compare and Contrast

(1) What were the differences between Angelo and Freda?

A. Angelo was selfish and Freda was generous.

B. Angelo felt sorry for himself and Freda felt sorry herself.

C. Angelo felt sorry for Freda and Freda felt sorry for only herself.

D. There was no difference between the two.

(2) How were Freda's feelings similar at the beginning of the story compared to the end of the story?

A. At the beginning of the story she was happy, but at the end of the story she was miserable.

B. At the beginning of the story she was miserable, but at the end of the story she was happy.

C. She was miserable at the beginning of the story and miserable at the end of the story.

D. Freda was happy at the beginning of the story and happy at the end of the story.

(3) How did the ocean differ at the beginning of the story compared to the end?

A. At the beginning of the story the ocean was calm and peaceful, but at the end of the story the ocean was rough and choppy.

B. At the beginning of the story the ocean was rough and choppy, but at the end of the story the ocean was calm and peaceful.

C. At the beginning of the story the ocean was fresh and salty, but at the end of the story the ocean was fresh and pure.

D. At the beginning of the story the ocean was fresh and pure, but at the end of the story the ocean was salty.

FORMATIVE ASSESSMENT:
Chronological Order

(1) Which event from the story happened AFTER Angelo saw the crying woman?

A. Angelo became a hard worker.

B. Angelo walked down from the mountains to the seashore.

C. Angelo dug caves.

D. Angelo built a mansion of salt blocks.

(2) What is the LAST event in the story?

A. Angelo walked along the seashore.

B. The crying woman began walking to her cave.

C. Angelo built the woman a beautiful mansion.

D. The ocean became salty due to the woman's tears.

(3) Place the events in chronological order.

1. *The salt dissolved into the ocean.*

2. *The crying woman returned to her cave.*

3. *Angelo agreed to build a beautiful house for the woman.*

4. *Angelo walked to the seashore.*

A. 3, 1, 2, 4

B. 4, 3, 1, 2

C. 1, 2, 3, 4

D. 3, 4, 2, 1

FORMATIVE ASSESSMENT:
Author's Purpose and Perspective

(1) The author most likely views Freda as being

    A. a happy and contented person.

    B. a sad and greedy person.

    C. a happy and selfish person.

    D. a cheerful and selfish person.

(2) What is the most likely reason the author wrote this story?

    A. to entertain the reader with a folktale of how the ocean became salty

    B. to tell the reader the true story of how the ocean became salty

    C. to convince the reader that the ocean is salty

    D. to compare how the ocean was different at the end of the story from the beginning of the story

(3) Which word below best describes the author's view of Angelo?

    A. withdrawn

    B. concerned

    C. regretful

    D. hysterical

(4) Which word best characterizes the overall tone of the passage?

    A. tragic

    B. entertaining

    C. scary

    D. frightening

FORMATIVE ASSESSMENT:
Word Analysis

(1) Read the sentence from the story.

Freda's tears eventually washed all of her house into the ocean.

In which of the following sentences does *washed* have the same meaning as in the sentence above?

A. The children *washed* the big, fluffy dog.

B. The man and woman *washed* the filthy windows of the building.

C. The swift river *washed* the bridge away.

D. The children *washed* in the lake.

(2) What does the word *beautiful* mean?

A. full of or having beauty

B. act of wanting beauty

C. without having beauty

D. state of having little beauty

(3) Read the following sentence.

Angelo was a hard worker and he loved to wander the land and help other people.

The word *worker* means

A. to make work.

B. state of work.

C. full of work.

D. a person who works.

FORMATIVE ASSESSMENT:
Context Clues

(1) Read the sentence from the story.

She told Angelo that she was tired of living in the subterranean cave.

As used in the sentence above, the word *subterranean* means

A. underground.

B. above ground.

C. sun-drenched.

D. threatening.

(2) Read the sentence from the story.

As Freda cried, her tears began to dissolve the salt and wash the house away.

What is the best meaning of the word *dissolve* as used in the sentence?

A. solidify

B. bake

C. liquefy

D. heat

(3) Read the sentence from the story.

Freda's tears eventually washed all of her house into the ocean.

What is the best meaning of the word *eventually* as used in the above sentence?

A. in time

B. never

C. formerly

D. already

FORMATIVE ASSESSMENT:
Synonyms and Antonyms

1 Which two words have nearly the OPPOSITE meaning?

A. bright/brilliant

B. giant/huge

C. crying/giggling

D. dark/gloomy

2 Which two words are MOST SIMILAR in meaning?

A. brick/block

B. white/black

C. wander/remain

D. dissolve/solidify

3 Which two words have nearly the OPPOSITE meaning?

A. seashore/beach

B. cave/cavern

C. mountain/valley

D. ocean/sea

4 Which two words are MOST SIMILAR in meaning?

A. promise/pledge

B. built/destroy

C. cry/laugh

D. salty/sweet

The Blind Poet

Three or four hundred years after the Trojan War, there lived a poor blind poet named Homer. Homer wandered about from place to place. As he walked he played upon his lyre, a musical instrument somewhat like a small harp. As Homer roamed, he recited wonderful verses which told about the adventures of the Greek heroes and their great deeds during the Trojan War. The Trojan War is believed by some to be a ten year war between Greece and Troy.

Stories were told that this elderly blind man had not always been poor and blind. It was said that having embarked by mistake upon a ship manned by pirates, Homer not only had been robbed of all his wealth and blinded, but had been left upon a lonely shore.

By some happy chance, poor Homer found his way to a part of the country where there were towns and villages. Homer soon won many friends. Instead of spending all his time weeping over his troubles, Homer tried to think of some way in which he could earn his living, and at the same time give pleasure to others. He soon found that reciting the heroic poems of the past brought joy to all who listened. These heroic poems focused on great Greek heroes.

As the people in those days had no books, no schools, and no televisions, these poems seemed very wonderful.

Little by little Homer turned them into verses so grand and beautiful that we admire them still. As he wandered from place to place, old and young crowded around him to listen to his tales. Some young people were so struck by the tales that they followed Homer everywhere, until they too could repeat them. This was quite easy to do because Homer had put them into the most beautiful language the world had ever known. As soon as these young men and women had learned a few of the tales, they too began to travel from place to place, telling the tales to all they met. This is how Homer's verses became known throughout all of Greece.

The Greeks who could recite Homer's poems eventually went to the islands, stopping at every place where Greek was spoken. Other youths learned the poems. Although the poems were not written down for many years, they were constantly recited and sung, and thus kept alive in the memory of the people. As for Homer, their author, we know little about him. We are told that he lived to be very old. Homer remained poor as long as he lived. He continued to earn his living by reciting his poems. Although he lived in poverty in life, he was greatly honored after his death. His two great heroic poems—the Iliad, which told all about the Trojan War, and the Odyssey, which told how the hero Ulysses sailed about for ten years on his way home from Troy—were finally written down, and kept so carefully that they can still be read today.

So many people admired these poems that some years after Homer's death an attempt was made to find out more about him and about the place where he was born.

Fifty cities claimed the honor of giving him birth. Although it was never known for certain where he was born, most people thought the Island of Chios was his birthplace. The Greek towns, wishing to show how much they admired the works of Homer, sent yearly gifts to this place, in honor of the grandest poet the world has ever known.

FORMATIVE ASSESSMENT:
Main Idea

(1) What would be a good title for this passage?

A. The Most Famous Poet of Greece

B. All People Should Become Poets

C. How to Write Poetry

D. Beautiful Poems

(2) The central point of the passage is

A. to tell about the poet Homer.

B. to tell why people in Greece enjoyed poetry.

C. to tell how dangerous sea travel was years ago.

D. to tell how Homer became blind.

(3) The primary purpose of the first paragraph of the passage is

A. to introduce the reader to Homer.

B. to introduce the reader to Greek poetry.

C. to tell the reader how Homer became blind.

D. to tell the reader about the daily life of Homer.

(4) The primary purpose of the last paragraph of the passage is

A. to tell of the great poems of Homer.

B. to tell of the Greek Islands.

C. to tell about famous poets of Greece.

D. to tell how proud the Greeks were of Homer.

FORMATIVE ASSESSMENT:
Supporting Details

1 Which detail from the passage helps show how much the Greeks enjoyed Homer's poetry?

    A. Homer had the most beautiful voice in Greece.

    B. As the people in those days had no books, no schools, and no televisions, these poems seemed very wonderful.

    C. As he wandered from place to place, old and young crowded around him to listen to his tales.

    D. Little by little Homer turned them into beautiful verses.

2 How did Homer become blind?

    A. He was in a boating accident.

    B. He had a disease.

    C. He was born blind.

    D. He was blinded by pirates.

3 When did Homer become a poet?

    A. before the Trojan War

    B. before he boarded the boat with pirates

    C. after the pirates left him on the shore

    D. after the young and old came to hear him recite poems

4 Where were gifts sent after Homer died?

    A. to the Island of Chios

    B. to the pirates

    C. to the Trojans

    D. to Rome

FORMATIVE ASSESSMENT:
Inferences

1. Why did Homer become more popular over time?

   A. Homer's poems were written down and sold to visitors.

   B. Homer's poems were retold by many storytellers and the people who heard the poems liked them.

   C. Homer became rich because of his poems.

   D. Homer's poetry made people sad.

2. Based on information in the passage, which is the most accurate statement regarding Homer?

   A. Homer sat around feeling sorry for himself after he became blind.

   B. Homer felt he could not earn a living because he was old.

   C. Homer expected other people to write poems for him.

   D. Homer continued to improve his poems to make the poems better.

3. The reader can infer that Homer was

   A. lazy.

   B. arrogant.

   C. dishonest.

   D. resourceful.

4. Why did over 50 cities claim to be Homer's birthplace?

   A. Each city was proud of Homer and wanted to claim being the place where he was born.

   B. Each city wanted to disrespect Homer.

   C. Each city wanted to laugh at Homer.

   D. The city would become famous for being the place where Homer died.

FORMATIVE ASSESSMENT:
Cause and Effect

1 Homer began reciting poems

 A. because there were no books or schools.

 B. because he was blind.

 C. because he needed to earn a living.

 D. because he thought poetry should be repeated.

2 Homer lost his wealth due to

 A. giving it to less fortunate people.

 B. being robbed by townspeople.

 C. being robbed by pirates.

 D. the Trojan War.

3 People enjoyed the poems Homer recited because

 A. the poems were easy to read.

 B. the poems were shown on television.

 C. the poems entertained people.

 D. the poems were easy to remember.

4 Young people followed Homer so that

 A. they could hear his poems about the Greek Gods.

 B. they could read his books.

 C. they could enjoy the gifts he received.

 D. they could learn the poems and eventually repeat them from memory.

FORMATIVE ASSESSMENT:
Compare and Contrast

1 According to the passage, Homer's life was different after he met the pirates. Which sentence describes how Homer's life was different?

A. Before he met the pirates Homer was a successful poet; after he met the pirates he was not a successful poet.

B. Before he met the pirates Homer could see; after he met the pirates he was blind.

C. Before he met the pirates Homer was happy; after he met the pirates he was sad.

D. Before he met the pirates Homer fought in the Trojan War; after he met the pirates he recited poetry.

2 How were Homer and the young poets alike?

A. Homer and the young poets made people happy by reciting poetry.

B. Homer and the young poets were poor.

C. Homer and the young poets were blind.

D. Homer and the young poets enjoyed wandering the world.

3 How were Homer's poems different early in his career compared to later in his career?

A. Early in his career his poems were not as grand as later in his career.

B. Early in his career his poems were grand and later they were not.

C. Early in his career his poems were the same as later in the career.

D. Early in his career his poems focused on nature; later in his career he focused on the Trojan War.

FORMATIVE ASSESSMENT:
Chronological Order

(1) According to the passage, which event happened FIRST?

   A. People claimed their cities to be Homer's birthplace.

   B. Greek townspeople sent gifts to the Island of Chios.

   C. Homer was blinded by pirates.

   D. The Trojan War occurred.

(2) What happened AFTER Homer was robbed and blinded but BEFORE he began reciting poems?

   A. He fought in the Trojan War.

   B. He was left on a lonely shore.

   C. He was honored as being a great poet.

   D. He boarded a boat with pirates.

(3) What is the LAST event that happened in the passage?

   A. Homer earned money reciting poems and singing songs.

   B. Homer returned to his hometown.

   C. Homer became blind.

   D. Greek townspeople sent gifts to the Island of Chios.

(4) What happened AFTER Homer began wandering the land reciting poems?

   A. The pirates blinded him.

   B. He became rich and famous.

   C. He returned to the city where he was originally born.

   D. People followed him and learned to recite the same poems.

FORMATIVE ASSESSMENT:
Author's Purpose and Perspective

① With which statement would the author of *The Blind Poet* most likely agree?

    A. Homer was a determined man.

    B. Homer was a man full of self-pity.

    C. Homer was a selfish man.

    D. Homer was a dishonest man.

② The author would most likely believe the young poets followed Homer because

    A. Homer made lots of money.

    B. Homer was famous.

    C. they wanted to learn how to recite the poems like Homer.

    D. they wanted to help Homer.

③ The most likely reason the author wrote this passage was to

    A. explain how to be a great poet.

    B. inform the reader about a great poet.

    C. persuade the reader that Homer was the greatest poet who ever lived.

    D. persuade the reader that war is wrong.

④ Which word best characterizes how the author feels about Homer?

    A. jealous

    B. admiration

    C. disrespect

    D. delight

FORMATIVE ASSESSMENT:
Word Analysis

(1) Read the following sentence.
As Homer roamed, he recited wonderful verses which told about the adventures of the Greek heroes and their great deeds during the Trojan War.
The word recited means

   A. told from memory.

   B. identified specifically.

   C. spelled correctly.

   D. named specifically.

(2) What does *heroic* mean as used in the following sentence?
These heroic poems focused on great Greek heroes.

   A. having or displaying qualities of a coward

   B. having or displaying qualities of a hero

   C. someone acting as an informer

   D. someone who is disloyal

(3) What does *musical* mean as used in the following sentence?
As he walked he played upon his lyre, a musical instrument somewhat like a small harp.

   A. of or pertaining to music

   B. a song sung by a musician

   C. place for music

   D. to play music again

FORMATIVE ASSESSMENT:
Context Clues

(1) Read the sentence below from the passage.
So many people admired these poems that some years after Homer's death an attempt was made to find out more about him and about the place where he was born.
In this sentence *attempt* means

   A. pioneer.

   B. effort.

   C. challenge.

   D. struggle.

(2) Read the sentence from the story.
So many people admired these poems that some years after Homer's death an attempt was made to find out more about him and about the place where he was born.
What does the word *admired* mean as used in the above sentence?

   A. regarded with sadness

   B. regarded with anticipation

   C. regarded with regret

   D. regarded with wonder and delight

(3) Read this sentence from the passage.
Some young people were struck by the poems.
What does the word *struck* mean as used in the above sentence?

   A. hit

   B. find unexpectedly

   C. affected

   D. walked out

FORMATIVE ASSESSMENT:
Synonyms and Antonyms

(**1**) Which two words have nearly the SAME meaning?

    A. wonderful/moral

    B. wonderful/noble

    C. wonderful/decent

    D. wonderful/superb

(**2**) Which two words are SIMILAR in meaning?

    A. focus/concentration

    B. focus/edge

    C. focus/rim

    D. focus/frame

(**3**) Which two words have nearly the SAME meaning?

    A. grand/great

    B. grand/poor

    C. grand/ordinary

    D. grand/humble

(**4**) Which two words are OPPOSITE in meaning?

    A. constantly/continually

    B. constantly/always

    C. constantly/seldom

    D. constantly/regularly

Pandora and the Golden Box
A GREEK MYTH

Once long ago, people had no fire to use to cook or keep warm. A man named Prometheus knew the Mighty Ones kept their fire on the mountaintop in a great fire pit. Prometheus snuck up to the fire pit and took a few embers. He then ran from the mountaintop and shared the fire with the people of the earth.

Several days later Zeus, the king of the Mighty Ones, looked down from his mountaintop home and saw fires burning and people enjoying the warmth. Zeus became very angry because he did not want people to have fire. He thought only the Mighty Ones should be allowed to have fire.

"Who has done this?" he asked.

Someone answered, "Prometheus!"

"What!" he cried. "Well, I will punish him! Let those puny men keep their fire. I will make them ten times more miserable than they were before they had it."

Of course it would be easy enough to deal with Prometheus at any time, so Zeus was in no great hurry. Zeus made up his mind to bother mankind first. He thought of a plan for doing it in a very strange, roundabout way.

Zeus ordered a beautiful golden box made. He placed thousands of horrible creatures inside the box. Zeus's sister, Hestia knew what Zeus intended and she placed one other creature in the box without Zeus knowing it.

"Now," said Zeus, "I will give this as a gift to a curious person."

Zeus knew that Pandora was the perfect person to receive the box. She was beautiful, had a pleasant voice, good manners, and a kind heart. But more than anything, Pandora was curious.

One morning Zeus knocked on Pandora's door and gave her the golden box. Zeus told her the box held many wonderful things. Zeus's sister, Hestia, had accompanied him to Pandora's house. She warned Pandora to never, never open it, or look at the things inside the box. As soon as Zeus and Hestia left Pandora's house, Pandora started to think about what might be in the box.

"There must be jewels in the box," Pandora said to herself.

Then she thought of how they would add to her beauty if only she could wear them.

"Why did Zeus give them to me if I should never use them or look at them?" she asked herself.

The more she thought about the golden box, the more curious she was to see what was in it. Every day she took it down from the shelf and felt the lid. Pandora tried to look inside the beautiful golden box without opening it.

"Why should I care what Hestia told me?" she thought to herself. "She is not beautiful and jewels would be of no use to her. I think that I will look inside the box. Hestia will never know. Nobody else will ever know."

She opened the lid slightly, just enough to peep inside. All at once there was a whirring and rustling sound. Before she could shut it, ten thousand strange creatures with horrible faces and gaunt, dreadful forms flew out of the box. There were things that nobody in all the world had ever seen. The creatures fluttered about the room for awhile and then flew away to find new homes with people.

These horrible creatures that had emerged from the beautiful, golden box were diseases and worries. Up to that time, mankind had not experienced sickness or worries of any kind.

These creatures flew into every house. Without anyone seeing them, they settled down in the hearts of men, women, and children. These creatures put an end to people's joy. Ever since that day they have been flitting and creeping, unseen and unheard bringing pain and sorrow into every household.

However, Pandora had not shut the lid tightly. A beautiful creature crept out of the box. Pandora watched in amazement as the beautiful creature emerged.

"Who are you?" asked Pandora in awe.

The tiny creature said, "I am Hope! Even though all the terrible diseases and worries escaped the box, I can still make the world a happy place. Where there is sadness, I will spread joy. Where there is disease, I will spread hope." Hope then flew out of Pandora's window and began helping all the people of the earth.

FORMATIVE ASSESSMENT:
Main Idea

(1) What would be another good title for this story?

A. The Little Bottle of Horrors

B. Pandora's Curiosity

C. Pandora and the Foolish Girl

D. Hope

(2) What is the main idea of the second paragraph?

A. Zeus was happy people had fire.

B. Zeus was angry people had fire.

C. Zeus wanted to give people fire.

D. Zeus wanted people to give him fire.

(3) What is the main idea of the last paragraph?

A. There was still a possibility that mankind could be happy.

B. Mankind was doomed to be miserable.

C. Hope did not want to help mankind.

D. Pandora was convinced mankind could help themselves.

(4) The author's primary point is

A. curiosity can cause harm.

B. people should not have fire.

C. Zeus was an evil being.

D. beautiful boxes are not good gifts.

FORMATIVE ASSESSMENT:
Supporting Details

(1) Which event did not happen in the story?

  A. Zeus knocked on Pandora's door and gave her the golden box.

  B. As soon as Zeus left Pandora's house, Pandora started to think about what might be in the box.

  C. Every day Pandora took the box down from the shelf and felt the lid.

  D. Zeus thought of a plan for helping mankind in a very strange, roundabout way.

(2) How did mankind obtain fire?

  A. Zeus gave fire to mankind.

  B. Mankind found fire.

  C. Pandora released fire from the box.

  D. Prometheus gave fire to mankind.

(3) Why did Zeus give Pandora the box?

  A. Zeus thought Pandora was the most beautiful woman in the world.

  B. Zeus thought Pandora was too curious and she would eventually open the box.

  C. Pandora had wanted a beautiful box.

  D. Zeus gave Pandora the box so she would release Hope.

(4) According to the story, how did disease get into the world?

  A. Zeus released diseases into the world.

  B. Prometheus released diseases into the world.

  C. Pandora released diseases into the world.

  D. Mankind released diseases into the world.

STORY SET 3

FORMATIVE ASSESSMENT:
Inferences

1 The reader can infer

   A. Zeus is using Pandora's curiosity to hurt mankind.

   B. Zeus dislikes mankind.

   C. Zeus does not want to help mankind.

   D. All of the above are correct.

2 The last creature to come out of the box was named Hope because

   A. she had the power to hurt mankind.

   B. Hope was afraid of Pandora.

   C. Zeus named her Hope.

   D. she had the power to help mankind.

3 The author implies

   A. although disease and worries were unleashed upon the earth, mankind would be alright because of Hope.

   B. mankind will not be safe.

   C. mankind does not care about disease and worries.

   D. mankind does not care about Hope.

4 How did Pandora probably feel upon seeing Hope at the end of the story?

   A. Pandora thought she was an evil creature.

   B. Pandora felt that mankind would be safe.

   C. Pandora thought Hope could not help mankind.

   D. Pandora was afraid Zeus would not allow Hope to help mankind.

FORMATIVE ASSESSMENT:
Cause and Effect

1. Why did Zeus order the golden box?

   A. Zeus was annoyed that people were happy and content.

   B. Zeus knew Pandora would purposely let the creatures out.

   C. Zeus was annoyed that Hestia wanted him to spare mankind.

   D. Zeus knew Pandora was greedy and wanted to give her jewels.

2. Why did Pandora want to open the box?

   A. She thought the box might contain jewels that would add to her beauty.

   B. She thought a treasure would be inside that would make her rich.

   C. She wanted to do the opposite of what Hestia told her to do.

   D. She wanted to obey Zeus.

3. What caused Zeus to choose Pandora to receive the box?

   A. Zeus hated Pandora because she was curious.

   B. Zeus wanted to make Pandora miserable.

   C. Zeus wanted Pandora to allow Hope to escape from the box.

   D. Zeus knew Pandora was curious and she would not be able to resist opening the box.

4. Why did Hestia place Hope in the golden box?

   A. She wanted to help mankind.

   B. She wanted to hurt mankind.

   C. She knew Hope needed a new home.

   D. She thought Pandora would like Hope.

FORMATIVE ASSESSMENT:
Compare and Contrast

1. How was Hope different than the other creatures that emerged from the box?

    A. Hope spread joy; the other creatures spread disease and worry.

    B. Hope spread disease; the other creatures spread joy.

    C. Neither Hope nor the other creatures spread joy.

    D. Hope and the creatures offered to spread joy and hope throughout the world.

2. How were the first creatures that flew from the golden box different from the last creature?

    A. The first creatures were good and the last creature was evil.

    B. All the creatures that flew from the box were good.

    C. All the creatures that flew from the box were evil.

    D. The first creatures were evil and the last creature was good.

3. How were Zeus and Prometheus different?

    A. Zeus believed that mankind should have fire and Prometheus believed mankind should not have fire.

    B. Prometheus believed that mankind should have fire and Zeus believed mankind should not have fire.

    C. Zeus believed Pandora should have the golden box and Prometheus believed Pandora should not have the golden box.

    D. Prometheus believed Pandora should have the golden box and Zeus believed Pandora should not have the golden box.

FORMATIVE ASSESSMENT:
Chronological Order

(1) Which event happened AFTER Pandora opened the box?

    A. Mankind did not experience any diseases or worries.

    B. Pandora opened the box slightly.

    C. Man became sick and worried.

    D. Hestia was very sad that Pandora had allowed Hope to escape.

(2) Which event occurred LAST in the story?

    A. Pandora opened the box.

    B. Hope escaped from the box.

    C. The creatures spread diseases and worries.

    D. Zeus gave Pandora a golden box.

(3) What happened immediately AFTER Zeus put the creatures in the box?

    A. Prometheus stole the fire.

    B. Prometheus gave the fire to man.

    C. Zeus gave the box to Pandora.

    D. Hestia placed another creature in the box.

(4) According to the story, AFTER Pandora opened the golden box, what event occurred next?

    A. Zeus became angry.

    B. The creatures flew out of the golden box.

    C. Pandora stopped the creatures from leaving the golden box.

    D. Hope flew out of the golden box.

FORMATIVE ASSESSMENT:
Author's Purpose and Perspective

(1) The author probably viewed Hope as being

A. unselfish.

B. rude.

C. disagreeable.

D. humorous.

(2) With which statement would the author of *Pandora and the Golden Box* MOST LIKELY agree?

A. Curiosity can cause harm.

B. Be nice to others and others will be nice to you.

C. Always look before crossing the street.

D. Judge yourself before you judge others.

(3) The author included curiosity as one of Pandora's character traits

A. so Pandora would be interesting.

B. so it would be believable that Pandora would open the golden box.

C. so readers would dislike Pandora.

D. so Pandora would not open the golden box.

(4) The author MOST LIKELY viewed Pandora as

A. adventurous.

B. nosy.

C. concerned.

D. quiet.

FORMATIVE ASSESSMENT:
Word Analysis

1 Read the sentence from the story.

She opened the lid slightly, just enough to peep inside.

What does the word *slightly* mean?

A. a little

B. to a large degree

C. not at all

D. greatly

2 Read the sentence from the story.

Up to that time, mankind had not experienced sickness or worries of any kind.

What does the word *sickness* mean?

A. not sick

B. to call to be sick

C. without being sick

D. being sick

3 Read the following sentence.

Before she could shut it, ten thousand strange creatures with horrible faces and gaunt, dreadful forms flew out of the box.

What does the word *dreadful* mean?

A. make dread

B. state of dread

C. full of dread

D. a person who dreads

FORMATIVE ASSESSMENT:
Context Clues

(1) Read this sentence from the story.

Zeus made up his mind to bother mankind first.

As used in the sentence above, the word *bother* means

A. to help.

B. to assist.

C. to annoy.

D. to support.

(2) Read the sentence from the story.

Prometheus snuck up to the fire pit and took a few embers.

As used in the sentence above, the word *embers* means

A. coals.

B. blocks.

C. sticks.

D. slabs.

(3) Which word could the author have used instead of the word *accompanied* in the sentence below?

Zeus's sister, Hestia, had accompanied him to Pandora's house.

A. complemented

B. associated

C. sprinted

D. escorted

FORMATIVE ASSESSMENT:
Synonyms and Antonyms

(1) Read this sentence from the story.

The creatures fluttered about the room for awhile and then flew away to find new homes with people.

Which word means almost the SAME as *fluttered*?

A. flapped

B. ran

C. clunked

D. staggered

(2) Read the sentence from the story.

These horrible creatures that had emerged from the beautiful, golden box were diseases and worries.

Which word means the OPPOSITE of *emerged*?

A. appeared

B. retreated

C. materialized

D. noted

(3) Read the sentence from the story.

Let those puny men keep their fire.

Which word means almost the SAME as *puny*?

A. weak

B. strong

C. thin

D. heavy

The Oak Tree

Sing for the oak tree,
The king of the wood.
Sing for the oak tree,
That grows green and good.
That grows broad and branching
Within the forest shade,
That grows now, and yet shall grow,
Its leaves are a lovely jade.

The oak tree was an acorn once,
And fell upon the earth.
And sun and showers nourished it,
And gave the oak tree birth.
The little sprouting oak tree!
Two leaves it had at first,
The sun and showers had nourished it,
Then out the branches burst.

The little sapling oak tree!
Its root was like a thread,
Till the kindly earth had nourished it;
Then out it freely spread.
On this side and on that side
It grappled with the ground.
And in the ancient, broken rock,
Its firmest footing found.

The winds came, and the rain fell,
The gusty tempest blew.
All were friends to the oak tree,
And stronger yet it grew.
The boy that saw the acorn fall,
He's older now and gray;
But the oak is still a thriving tree,
And strengthens every day.

FORMATIVE ASSESSMENT:
Main Idea

1 What is the poem *The Oak Tree* mainly about?

    A. a young oak tree

    B. an old oak tree

    C. an acorn growing and becoming a tree

    D. an acorn in different kinds of weather

2 What would be the best title for this poem?

    A. Little Acorn, Big Tree

    B. Acorn

    C. The Old Oak Tree

    D. The Boy Who Likes Acorns

3 What is the main idea of the third stanza?

    A. an acorn falling from the tree

    B. the growth of a young tree

    C. the growth of a young boy

    D. an adult tree and its strength

4 What is the main idea of the fourth stanza?

    A. a man and the sadness he feels

    B. a tree that is still growing stronger

    C. the acorn falling from the tree

    D. the death of the oak tree

FORMATIVE ASSESSMENT:
Supporting Details

(1) Which detail from the poem helps show how fragile and small the oak tree was at one time?

   A. The little sapling oak tree!

   B. Its root was like a thread.

   C. The kindly earth had nourished it.

   D. Then out it freely spread.

(2) What color are the oak tree's leaves?

   A. brown

   B. golden

   C. jade

   D. yellow-green

(3) What helped the oak tree grow?

   A. the sun and showers

   B. the shade and woods

   C. the rain and woods

   D. the acorn and rain

(4) How many leaves did the oak tree have in the second stanza?

   A. one

   B. two

   C. three

   D. four

FORMATIVE ASSESSMENT:
Inferences

1 Where is the setting of the poem?

A. the woods

B. the city

C. a small village

D. a large lake

2 The reader can assume that

A. there are lots of oak trees in the forest.

B. the oak tree grows for a long time.

C. the oak tree does not need much water to survive.

D. the oak tree does not need sunlight to grow.

3 The poem suggests

A. oak trees live longer than people.

B. oak trees live for a few years.

C. oak trees live for over ten thousand years.

D. oak trees live less than one year.

4 The reader can infer

A. the boy has grown into an old man.

B. the boy has grown up and now has a son of his own.

C. the oak tree was cut down for furniture.

D. the oak tree died of old age.

FORMATIVE ASSESSMENT:
Cause and Effect

1. In the second stanza, what caused the oak tree's branches to burst outward?

   A. The small boy watered it.

   B. The ancient rock pushed the branches outward.

   C. The rich soil nourished it.

   D. The sun and showers nourished it.

2. What was the effect of time passing?

   A. Several other oak trees began to grow.

   B. The boy became a man.

   C. The sun began to shine.

   D. The rain eventually stopped.

3. What was the effect of the rain and sun on the acorn?

   A. The oak tree began to grow.

   B. The acorn rotted away.

   C. The acorn doubled in size.

   D. It had no effect.

4. Why does the author think the oak tree should be honored?

   A. The author thinks the oak tree is a magnificent tree.

   B. The oak tree is the boy's favorite tree.

   C. The oak tree grows forever.

   D. The oak tree is the color of jade.

FORMATIVE ASSESSMENT:
Compare and Contrast

1 How did the oak tree change in the poem?

    A. It began as a little acorn and eventually became a strong tree.

    B. It did not change.

    C. It started as a small tree and became a large tree.

    D. It was a large tree throughout the poem.

2 How did the boy who saw the acorn fall change in the poem?

    A. He became greedy.

    B. He grew older.

    C. He became carefree.

    D. He did not change.

3 How were the boy and the oak tree different?

    A. The oak tree continued growing larger and the boy became a man and stopped growing.

    B. The boy continued growing and the oak tree stopped growing.

    C. The oak tree and the boy continued growing.

    D. The oak tree and the boy stopped growing.

4 How were the boy and the oak tree similar?

    A. Both the boy and the tree grew when they were young.

    B. Both the boy and the tree felt the wind during the storm.

    C. The boy and the tree needed soil to grow.

    D. The boy and the tree did not need water to grow.

FORMATIVE ASSESSMENT:
Chronological Order

1. What happened BEFORE the root grew freely?

   A. The earth nourished it.

   B. The tree was planted by the boy.

   C. The tree was moved to another location.

   D. The wind blew it.

2. What happened BEFORE the acorn began to grow?

   A. The boy stepped on the acorn and cracked it open.

   B. The man planted the acorn.

   C. The man was walking in the woods.

   D. The acorn received sunlight and rain.

3. What was the oak tree doing at the end of the poem?

   A. The oak tree had stopped growing.

   B. The oak tree was still growing.

   C. The oak tree had two leaves.

   D. The branches of the oak tree had began to droop.

4. Where was the acorn BEFORE it fell upon the earth?

   A. hanging from the tree

   B. on the ground

   C. by the lake

   D. in the boy's pocket

FORMATIVE ASSESSMENT:
Author's Purpose and Perspective

(1) How did the author probably feel about the oak tree?

   A. The author thought the oak tree was a great tree.

   B. The author did not like the oak tree.

   C. The author thought the oak tree was not as good as other trees.

   D. The author thought the oak tree should be moved to a new location.

(2) Read the lines of poetry.
Sing for the oak tree,
The king of the wood
These lines of poetry indicate that the author viewed the oak tree as

   A. a majestic tree.

   B. a pathetic tree.

   C. a common tree.

   D. a weak tree.

(3) With which statement would the author of *The Oak Tree* most likely agree?

   A. The oak tree was only one of many beautiful trees.

   B. It was amazing that the oak tree began life as a tiny acorn and grew into a huge tree.

   C. The oak tree was an excellent source of wood for furniture.

   D. The oak tree grew quickly in a short time.

FORMATIVE ASSESSMENT:
Word Analysis

1 Read the lines from the poem *The Oak Tree*.
Its root was like a thread,
Till the kindly earth had nourished it;
And in the ancient, broken rock,
Its firmest footing found.

What is meant by, *"Its firmest footing found"*?

A. The boy found firm footing.

B. The roots became firmly planted.

C. The roots became loose.

D. The boy found the roots loose.

2 Read the two lines from the poem *The Oak Tree*.
And sun and showers nourished it,
And gave the oak tree birth.
What does the word *nourished* mean?

A. to promote the development of

B. to stop the development of

C. to hinder the development of

D. to reverse the development of

3 What does the word *kindly* mean in the phrase?
Till the kindly earth had nourished it;

A. in the worst way

B. in a kind manner

C. in a happy way

D. in a gentle way

STORY SET 4

FORMATIVE ASSESSMENT:
Context Clues

(1) Read this sentence from the story.
The gusty tempest blew.
What does the word *tempest* mean?

   A. storm

   B. riot

   C. uproar

   D. breeze

(2) Read the sentence from the poem.
Its leaves are a lovely jade.
The word *jade* means

   A. yellow in color.

   B. green in color.

   C. blue in color.

   D. brown in color.

(3) Read the sentence from the story.
Then out the branches burst.
What does the word *burst* mean in the sentence?

   A. sprang

   B. drifted

   C. poured

   D. stopped

FORMATIVE ASSESSMENT:
Synonyms and Antonyms

1 Which word pair has nearly the OPPOSITE meaning?

  A. strengthen/reinforce

  B. strengthen/increase

  C. strengthen/weaken

  D. strengthen/support

2 Which word pair has nearly the SAME meaning?

  A. spread/expand

  B. spread/withdraw

  C. spread/decrease

  D. spread/fold

3 Which word pair has nearly the OPPOSITE meaning?

  A. thriving/flourishing

  B. thriving/successful

  C. thriving/booming

  D. thriving/failing

4 Which word pair has nearly the SAME meaning?

  A. sprouting/budding

  B. sprouting/declining

  C. sprouting/wasting

  D. sprouting/moving

Dinosaur National Monument

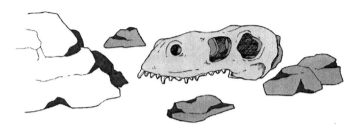

Located in Colorado and Utah, Dinosaur National Monument is a place to learn about fossils, enjoy nature, and spend time in outdoor activities. The following basic information is provided so visitors can plan their trip to Dinosaur National Monument. The 210,000 acres within the park will grab visitors' attention with its beauty, rugged wilderness, solitude, and silence. This is a place to relax and reflect, or hike, drive, and boat through the diverse landscapes. Enjoy!

What Does It Cost?

An entrance fee is charged only in the Dinosaur Quarry. The entrance fee is good for 7 days:

- $10 per family vehicle
- $5 per motorcycle ($10 with a passenger)
- $5 for an individual (hiker or bicycle)
- Special fees for commercial tours and buses apply. Call for an educational group entrance fee waiver or more detailed information.

Camping fees vary depending on the season and facilities. Be prepared to pay from $6.00 to $12.00 per night. Rates for the reservation-only group campsites at Split Mountain group campground are higher.

Fees and non-commercial river permits are required for private white water river trips on the Green and Yampa rivers within the park. For information on fees, equipment and experience requirements, and how to apply for the permit, call the park office.

What Kinds of Recreational Activities Are There to Do?

There are many recreational activities available at Dinosaur National Monument. Hiking trails are plentiful and hiking visitors are able to get close to nature. There are also white water boat trips. The boat trips may be the best way to see Dinosaur National Monument. In addition to experiencing the thrill of riding the rapids, visitors also get to see beautiful cliffs, awe-inspiring bighorn sheep and nature.

Fishing is also available. Visitors who fish must be aware that there are four endangered native fish that live in the rivers within the area. If an endangered fish is hooked by a fisherman, the fish must immediately be returned to the water. Catfish and pike are plentiful at the Green Yampa Rivers. Brown and rainbow trout are numerous in Jones Hole Creek. Jones Hole Creek is a perfect habitat for these fish. There are restrictions as to which types of tackle can be used at Jones Hole Creek. Fishermen who would like to fish within Dinosaur National Monument must have a fishing license and be familiar with the rules.

There are no swimming accommodations at Dinosaur National Monument due to the river water being cold with strong currents. However, there are swimming pools available close to the monument.

Mountain biking is a sport that is slowly growing in popularity at Dinosaur National Monument. Although there are no mountain bike trails in the monument, bikes can travel on the paved and unpaved roads in the monument. The roads are narrow and there are no bike paths. Mountain bikes are not allowed on any hiking trails or backcountry roads. There are several routes that mountain bikers can take that are enjoyable. One of the best mountain bike routes in the monument is the Island Park Road. The Island Park Road is 12 - 17 miles long one way and ends at a campground. It is unpaved, but well maintained, and an easy ride. Another

great bike route is the Echo Park Road. It is 13 miles long one way and ends at the Echo Park Campground (camping fee required). It is unpaved, rough and steep, and a tricky ride. The Yampa Bench Road is 51 miles long in the monument and an additional 20 miles or so to US 40. There are no campgrounds or water along this route. The road is unpaved, rough, and steep in several places, and is a very difficult ride. Good planning is necessary for this trip.

Can I Bring My Pets?

Bringing pets to the park may restrict visitors' activities. Pets are not allowed in the visitor centers, on any of the trails, in the backcountry, or in boats. Pets must be on a leash at all times. Visitors can keep their pets with them at their campsite. Sometimes people think they can hike a trail and their pet will be okay in the car. That is not the case, however. The daytime temperatures are warm and pets have suffered terribly by being kept in a hot car, even with the windows partially rolled down for ventilation.

Is the Park Crowded with People and Cars?

The number of people who visit Dinosaur National Monument during the summer is low compared to other parks and that is one of its charms. The Dinosaur Quarry may be crowded in the middle of the day. The rest of the park, however, is another story. There is always enough parking at the attractions. Campgrounds usually do not fill up. Without a doubt, Dinosaur National Monument is a wonderful park for silence, relaxation, and reflection.

What is Available for Children to Do?

Dinosaurs fascinate children. Therefore, a visit to the Dinosaur Quarry is exciting for most youngsters. The Quarry bookstore has a fine selection of books and educational items specifically for children.

There is a Junior Ranger program in which children can participate. However, it is not like the typical Junior Ranger programs at some other National Parks. Before children can participate in the program, their parents must sign a consent form. The program is more challenging and more time consuming. It is designed to involve both the child and parent and to be educational.

The Desert Voices Nature Trail has wayside signs along the trail that were designed by children, for children. This is an enjoyable walk for a family. Youngsters like to get out and do things, so a walk along any of the park's trails can be enjoyable for children.

Children love river trips. Tickets are available for purchase for a one-day or multi-day river trip. Tickets must be purchased prior to the river trip. A one-day or multi-day river trip will provide children experiences they will remember for the rest of their lives.

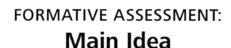

FORMATIVE ASSESSMENT:
Main Idea

(1) What would be a good title for this article?

A. Everything You Need to Know About Dinosaur National Monument

B. The Best National Parks to Visit

C. How to Find Dinosaur National Monument

D. Finding Dinosaurs

(2) What is the central point of the passage?

A. to provide information about how to take care of pets at Dinosaur National Monument

B. to provide information about fishing at Dinosaur National Monument

C. to provide information so visitors can plan their trip to Dinosaur National Monument

D. to provide information about swimming at Dinosaur National Monument

(3) What is the primary point of the section with the subheading *What is Available for Children to Do?*

A. to provide information about activities that children would enjoy participating in at Dinosaur National Monument

B. to provide information about the Junior Ranger program at Dinosaur National Monument

C. to provide information about the type of fishing tackle children need at Dinosaur National Monument

D. to provide information about the river trips that children would enjoy at Dinosaur National Monument

FORMATIVE ASSESSMENT:
Supporting Details

1. What kinds of recreational activities are there to do at Dinosaur National Monument?

   A. hiking, swimming, white water boat trips, fishing

   B. biking, swimming, white water boat trips, fishing

   C. white water boat trips, swimming, fishing

   D. hiking, biking, white water boat trips, fishing

2. Before fishing, a fisherman must have

   A. a fishing license.

   B. tackle.

   C. permission to fish in the lakes.

   D. a container to put the fish into after catching them.

3. Which statement about Dinosaur National Monument is not true?

   A. It costs ten dollars for a family to enter the park in a car.

   B. Hiking is available in Dinosaur National Monument.

   C. Swimming pools are plentiful in Dinosaur National Monument.

   D. Echo Park Road is a great road for bike riding.

4. Which detail supports the idea that pets should be brought to Dinosaur National Monument?

   A. Bringing pets to the park may restrict visitors' activities.

   B. Visitors can keep their pets with them at their campsite.

   C. Pets are not allowed in the visitor centers, on any of the park's trails, in the backcountry, or in boats.

   D. Pets may suffer terribly in the heat at Dinosaur National Monument.

FORMATIVE ASSESSMENT:
Inferences

(1) Why is it important for fishermen to release the fish that are endangered?

   A. so the endangered fish can reproduce

   B. so the endangered fish can be caught by other fishermen

   C. so the endangered fish can continue to swim with the other fish

   D. so the endangered fish can swim to new rivers

(2) Why were children selected to create the signs for the Desert Voices Nature Trail?

   A. The children did not charge for their work.

   B. Children enjoy seeing other children's creations.

   C. Children are more creative than adults.

   D. Children were the only people available to create the signs.

(3) Why do people enjoy visiting Dinosaur National Monument?

   A. Dinosaur National Monument is free to enter.

   B. Dinosaur National Monument provides free transportation to the park.

   C. Dinosaur National Monument has a variety of activities that people can enjoy.

   D. Dinosaur National Monument is the only park in the United States.

FORMATIVE ASSESSMENT:
Cause and Effect

(1)   Why must fishermen recognize the four endangered native fish?

   A. so they know which fish taste the best

   B. so they know which fish might bite

   C. so they know which fish should be released

   D. so they know which fish will live the longest

(2)   Why should pets not be brought to Dinosaur National Monument?

   A. There are many places within the park where the pets are not allowed.

   B. Pets could easily become lost.

   C. Pets are not allowed at campsites.

   D. There are many types of diseases that pets could become infected with at the park.

(3)   Why should people not visit Dinosaur Quarry in the middle of the day in the summer?

   A. Dinosaur Quarry offers many different activities in which people can participate.

   B. Dinosaur Quarry is too crowded in the middle of the day in the summer.

   C. The Dinosaur Quarry closes at noon in the summer.

   D. The Dinosaur Quarry does not allow visitors in the afternoon.

FORMATIVE ASSESSMENT:
Compare and Contrast

1 Compare the Dinosaur National Monument Junior Ranger program to the Junior Ranger programs at other National Parks.

   A. The Junior Ranger programs at other National Parks are more challenging and more time consuming than the Junior Ranger program at Dinosaur National Monument.

   B. The Junior Ranger program at Dinosaur National Monument is more challenging and time consuming than the Junior Ranger programs at other national parks.

   C. All the programs are the same.

   D. The Junior Ranger program at Dinosaur National Monument requires all children be at least 12 years old in order to participate.

2 Compare how Island Park Road and Yampa Bench Road are different.

   A. Yampa Bench Road is longer than Island Park Road.

   B. Island Park Road is longer than Yampa Bench Road.

   C. Yampa Bench Road has a campground, but Island Park Road does not have a campground.

   D. Yampa Bench Road has places to stop for water, but Island Park Road does not.

3 How is riding the rapids different than other activities at Dinosaur National Monument.

   A. Visitors get to see beautiful cliffs.

   B. Visitors get to see fish.

   C. Visitors get close to nature.

   D. Visitors get to enjoy warm temperatures.

FORMATIVE ASSESSMENT:
Chronological Order

(1) What must occur BEFORE a visitor can enter Dinosaur National Monument?

 A. Visitors must stop and get a park map.

 B. Visitors must pay an entrance fee.

 C. Visitors must rent a camping space.

 D. Visitors must leave before dark.

(2) What must occur BEFORE children can participate in the Junior Ranger program?

 A. The children's parents must sign a consent form.

 B. The children must pay a fee.

 C. The children must be willing to play sports.

 D. The children's parents must participate.

(3) What happens BEFORE a person goes on a river trip?

 A. The person must sign a consent form.

 B. The person must pack a lunch.

 C. A boat must be rented.

 D. A permit must be obtained.

FORMATIVE ASSESSMENT:
Author's Purpose and Perspective

(1) Why did the author write this article?

  A. to tell a story about Dinosaur National Monument

  B. to provide information about Dinosaur National Monument

  C. to persuade the reader that activities at Dinosaur National Monument are better than at other National Parks

  D. to describe what campgrounds look like at Dinosaur National Monument

(2) How would the author probably describe Dinosaur National Monument?

  A. ugly

  B. magnificent

  C. boring

  D. dangerous

(3) Which word best characterizes the overall tone of the passage?

  A. instructive

  B. sarcastic

  C. serious

  D. remorseful

FORMATIVE ASSESSMENT:
Word Analysis

1 Read the sentence from the passage.

Fees and non-commercial river permits are required for private white water river trips on the Green and Yampa rivers within the park.

The word *non-commercial* means

A. able to be commercial.

B. very small commercial.

C. not commercial.

D. extremely commercial.

2 Read the sentence from the passage.

Another great bike route is Echo Park Road. It is 13 miles long one way and ends at the Echo Park Campground (camping fee required). It is unpaved, rough and steep, and a tricky ride.

The word *unpaved* means

A. heavily paved.

B. not paved.

C. somewhat paved.

D. paved again.

3 Read the sentence from the passage.

Youngsters like to get out and do things, so a walk along any of the trails in the park can be enjoyable for children.

The word *enjoyable* means

A. one who enjoys.

B. not allowed to be enjoyed.

C. somewhat dreadful.

D. able to be enjoyed.

FORMATIVE ASSESSMENT:
Context Clues

(1) Read the following sentence.

The daytime temperatures are warm and pets have suffered terribly by being kept in a hot car, even with the windows partially rolled down for ventilation.

What does the word *ventilation* mean in the sentence?

A. dry heat

B. circulation of air

C. protection

D. security

(2) Read these sentences from the story.

Dinosaurs fascinate children. Therefore, a visit to the Dinosaur Quarry is exciting for most youngsters.

As used in the sentence above, the word *fascinate* means

A. interest.

B. repel.

C. bore.

D. exhaust.

(3) Read the sentences from the story.

Bringing pets to the park may restrict visitors' activities. Pets are not allowed in the visitor centers or on any of the trails.

What does the word *restrict* mean?

A. broaden

B. limit

C. promote

D. support

STORY SET 5

FORMATIVE ASSESSMENT:
Synonyms and Antonyms

1 Read the sentence from the passage.

Call for an educational group entrance fee waiver or more detailed information.

Which word most nearly means the OPPOSITE of *detailed*?

A. full

B. in depth

C. comprehensive

D. sketchy

2 Read the sentence from the passage.

This is a place to relax and reflect, or hike, drive, and boat through the diverse landscapes.

Which word most nearly means the SAME as *diverse*?

A. similar

B. opposite

C. varied

D. comparable

3 Read the sentence from the passage.

In addition to experiencing the thrill of riding the rapids, visitors also get to see beautiful cliffs, awe-inspiring bighorn sheep and nature.

Which word means nearly the SAME as *thrill*?

A. excitement

B. joy

C. boredom

D. sorrow

Juan and His Painted Hat

A TALE FROM THE PHILIPPINES

There once lived a man by the name of Juan who did nothing but trick people all the time. Once when he had only seventy pesos left in his pockets, he decided to play a trick on his friends and earn some money at the same time.

Juan decided he would use a hat to play the trick. For the trick, Juan bought a hat and painted it many different colors. The hat was beautiful when Juan finished with it.

In the town where Juan lived, there were only three stores. He went to each one and deposited twenty pesos, saying to each of the owners, "I will deposit twenty pesos in your store, and tomorrow afternoon I will bring some friends here with me. We will take some food or other items, but, in any case, I will see to it that the total amount of the things we take is not over the twenty pesos. Then, when we leave, do not ask me to pay you for the things. I will simply make a bow with my hat, and your store clerks should thank me with much courtesy. That mere bow with my hat is to be the payment. You may keep the twenty pesos, but you must also keep this little plan a secret."

The owners of the three stores promised.

The next day Juan was walking in the street with his painted hat on, when one of his friends met him.

"Hello, Juan!" exclaimed his friend, "Where did you get that funny hat?"

Juan looked serious and said, "Don't be foolish! Don't you know that this hat is the only means I have of earning a living?"

"Means of earning a living?" returned Juan's friend.

"Why, of course. I can go in any store, take anything I please, and pay for it with a mere bow of my hat."

By this time two other friends of Juan had come along, and they too were surprised to see what Juan had on his head. To convince them of the marvelous power of the hat, Juan took his friends to one of the stores. There they sat down, and Juan ordered some refreshments. They ate a large amount of food.

After they had eaten enough, Juan stood up, made a bow to the storeowner with his hat, and they all left. Then Juan and his friends visited another store where the same thing took place.

Juan's friends were very much astonished and each wished to own the wonderful hat. One offered him a thousand pesos for it. Another friend offered two thousand for the seemingly magical hat. Juan's third friend offered five thousand pesos. Juan, of course, was willing to sell it to the highest bidder. However, when the sale was about to be concluded, the buyer began to doubt the power of the hat. So he asked Juan to take him to another store to prove once more the power of the hat. Juan took his friend to the third store and the friend was now sure that the hat could really work wonders. So he paid Juan the five thousand pesos.

A few days later the friend who had bought the hat wanted to show it off. He invited several friends to go to the store with him. He took them to one of the stores and ordered some refreshments. When they had finished, the man bowed with his hat and started to leave.

"Thank you, sir!" said the owner of the store, "But where is my payment for the refreshments you have just eaten?"

The owner of the hat was astonished and thinking that perhaps he held the hat in the wrong way, or else his fingers were not on the right color, he turned the hat around. Then he made another bow. The owner of the shop became angry. The man, who had bought the hat from Juan, became excited, twirling the hat around, and holding it in many different ways, trying desperately to make it work. Finally, the shopkeeper threatened to have the man arrested if he did not pay. At about the same time, Juan walked into the store. He saw how upset his friend was and he immediately knew why his friend was so distressed. Juan started to think about what he had done to his friend. Suddenly Juan knew what he needed to do. He quickly paid the storeowner what his friend owed and shamefully admitted what he had done. Then Juan gave his friend back the five thousand pesos for the hat.

Although Juan's friend was very angry when he learned of the trick Juan had played, he knew he could not stay angry with Juan. After all, Juan had come forward and told the truth. Juan and his friend each learned a lesson.

FORMATIVE ASSESSMENT:
Main Idea

(1) What is the main idea of the story?

   A. Juan thought of a way to trick a friend out of money and when Juan realized he made a mistake he gave his friend his money back.

   B. Juan's friends decided to play a trick on him. His friends gave him a beautiful, painted hat that allowed Juan to get free items at the local stores.

   C. Juan thought of a way to trick a friend out of money. Even though Juan realized he had made a mistake, he refused to return the money to his friend.

   D. Juan sold his friend a magical hat. The magic would work only for Juan, so Juan returned his friends money.

(2) What would be a good title for this story?

   A. The Magical Hat

   B. The Man Who Learned a Valuable Lesson

   C. Juan Loves Money

   D. How to Play a Trick on Friends

(3) What is the main idea of the last paragraph?

   A. Juan knew he would continue to trick his friends.

   B. Juan's friend decided he would never trust Juan again.

   C. Juan and his friend refused to ever speak to each other again.

   D. Juan's friend forgave Juan for the trick.

FORMATIVE ASSESSMENT:
Supporting Details

1 Where is the setting of *Juan and His Painted Hat*?

   A. a department store

   B. a restaurant in Mexico

   C. a large city

   D. a small town

2 How did the man who bought the hat discover it was not magic?

   A. The man tried to use it in a store and it would not work.

   B. The store clerk said it was not a magic hat.

   C. The police told the man it was not a magic hat.

   D. Juan continued to maintain that the hat was magic.

3 Why did the shopkeepers allow Juan to tip his hat instead of pay for the items that Juan bought?

   A. Juan's hat was magic.

   B. Juan's friends were paying for the items that Juan bought.

   C. Juan had paid in advance for the items he bought.

   D. Juan told the shopkeepers he would pay for the items later.

4 In the story, what does Juan claim is unique about his hat?

   A. The hat is magic.

   B. The hat is painted brightly.

   C. The hat is expensive.

   D. The hat caused Juan's friend to become very angry.

FORMATIVE ASSESSMENT:
Inferences

(1) How did Juan trick his friend into buying the magic hat?

   A. Juan made his friend believe the hat would allow him to get things for free.

   B. Juan told his friend it was a very comfortable hat.

   C. Juan made his friend believe the hat was the most brightly painted hat in town.

   D. Juan made his friend believe that the hat would grant every wish.

(2) Why did the man who bought the hat from Juan twirl the hat around when it was time to pay the storekeeper?

   A. The man was nervous because he did not have any money.

   B. The man was trying to make the magic hat work.

   C. The man was angry that he had been tricked by Juan.

   D. The man was trying to get the shopkeeper to feel sorry for him.

(3) The reader of the story can assume that

   A. the shopkeepers were greedy men.

   B. Juan's friends were all foolish.

   C. Juan was an evil man.

   D. the man who bought the hat would be more careful before buying anything again.

FORMATIVE ASSESSMENT:
Cause and Effect

1. Why didn't the owner of the store have Juan arrested after Juan and his friends ate food and didn't pay?

   A. Juan was going to pay for the food later.

   B. Juan had paid in advance for the food.

   C. Juan's special hat allowed him to get the food free.

   D. The store owner was Juan's friend, so he did not charge Juan.

2. Why did Juan decide to trick his friends?

   A. Juan wanted to tease his friends.

   B. Juan thought the trick would be funny.

   C. Juan's friends enjoyed a good trick.

   D. Juan wanted money.

3. Why did Juan confess what he had done and return his friend's money?

   A. Juan never intended to keep his friend's money.

   B. Juan saw his friend was very upset and about to be arrested.

   C. Juan felt guilty from the moment he took the money from his friend.

   D. Juan's friend begged Juan to return the money.

FORMATIVE ASSESSMENT:
Compare and Contrast

(1) How is Juan DIFFERENT at the end of the story than at the beginning of the story?

   A. At the beginning of the story Juan is concerned about helping his friend. At the end of the story Juan does not want to help his friend.

   B. At the beginning of the story Juan wants to trick his friend into giving him money. At the end of the story Juan is sorry he tricked his friend.

   C. Juan is concerned about his friend at the beginning of the story. At the end of the story Juan is impatient with his friend.

   D. Juan does not change from the beginning of the story to the end of the story.

(2) How are the shopkeepers DIFFERENT than Juan?

   A. The shopkeepers are not trying to cheat Juan's friends out of money.

   B. The shopkeepers are much younger than Juan.

   C. The shopkeepers value the hat more than Juan.

   D. The shopkeepers enjoy tricking people.

(3) How are the shopkeepers and the police probably SIMILAR?

   A. They all believe that the man who bought the hat from Juan should pay for what he bought.

   B. They all believe Juan can make the hat work.

   C. They all believe the hat was too expensive.

   D. They all believe the man who bought the hat should sell it to someone else.

FORMATIVE ASSESSMENT:
Chronological Order

(1) Place the events in the correct order.

1. *Juan returned the 5,000 pesos.*

2. *Juan decided to play a trick on a friend and earn some money at the same time.*

3. *Juan realized he had made a mistake.*

4. *Juan gave the owners of the stores 20 pesos each.*

A. 1, 2, 3, 4

B. 4, 2, 3, 1

C. 2, 4, 3, 1

D. 3, 4, 2, 1

(2) After the store owner became angry at the man who had bought the hat from Juan, what happened next?

A. The shopkeeper called the police.

B. The man who bought the hat from Juan became angry.

C. The man who bought the hat from Juan became excited.

D. The shopkeeper refused to accept money from Juan.

(3) What happened FIRST in the story?

A. Juan apologized to his friend.

B. Juan painted his hat.

C. Juan took his friends to a restaurant.

D. Juan paid his friend back the money he owed him.

FORMATIVE ASSESSMENT:
Author's Purpose and Perspective

1. Why did the author write this story?

   A. to entertain the reader with a story about an intelligent man

   B. to entertain the reader with a story about a dishonest man who learns a lesson

   C. to persuade the reader to be careful of a friend's tricks

   D. to persuade the reader tricks can hurt people

2. The author most likely views the man who bought the hat as

   A. calm.

   B. dishonest.

   C. foolish.

   D. relaxed.

3. How would the author likely describe Juan's friends who did not buy the hat?

   A. insulting

   B. sarcastic

   C. frustrated

   D. lucky

STORY SET 6

FORMATIVE ASSESSMENT:
Word Analysis

1 Read this sentence from the story.
He quickly paid the storeowner what his friend owed and shamefully admitted what he had done.

What does the word *quickly* mean?

A. in a quick manner

B. to be quick again

C. not to be quick

D. after being quick

2 Read this sentence from the story.
He quickly paid the storeowner what his friend owed and shamefully admitted what he had done.

What does the word *shamefully* mean?

A. having no shame

B. capable of having shame

C. relating to shame

D. in a manner that is full of shame

3 Read this following sentence.
Another friend offered two thousand pesos for the seemingly magical hat.
What does the word *magical* mean?

A. to hope for magic

B. to believe in magic

C. a place for magic

D. of or relating to magic

FORMATIVE ASSESSMENT:
Context Clues

1 Read this sentence from the story.

He took his friends to one of the stores and ordered some refreshments.

As used in the sentence above, the word *refreshments* means

A. assorted light foods.

B. a banquet.

C. a feast.

D. a ceremonial dinner.

2 Read this sentence from the story.

The owner of the hat was astonished and thinking that perhaps he held the hat in the wrong way, or else his fingers were not on the right color, he turned the hat around.

As used in the sentence above, the word *astonished* means

A. incorrect.

B. surprised.

C. relieved.

D. dishonest.

3 Read this sentence from the story.

The man, who had bought the hat from Juan, became excited, twirling the hat around, trying desperately to make it work.

As used in the sentence above, the word *desperately* means

A. frantically.

B. calmly.

C. sadly.

D. worriedly.

STORY SET 6

FORMATIVE ASSESSMENT:
Synonyms and Antonyms

1 Read the following excerpt from *Juan and His Painted Hat*.

The owner of the shop became livid. Finally, the shopkeeper threatened to have the man arrested if he did not pay.

What is a SYNONYM for the word *livid*?

A. excited

B. angry

C. sad

D. happy

2 Which two words below are nearly OPPOSITE in meaning?

A. foolish/unwise

B. foolish/risky

C. foolish/sad

D. foolish/sensible

3 Which two words are ANTONYMS?

A. enough/sufficient

B. enough/adequate

C. enough/insufficient

D. plenty/ample

4 Which two words are ANTONYMS?

A. friends/pals

B. friends/comrades

C. friends/enemies

D. friends/buddies

Aunt Jemima's Quilt
–Samuel Minturn Peck

A miracle of gleaming dyes,
Blue, scarlet, beige and green;
Oh never before by human eyes
Such gorgeous colors were seen!
So grandly was its plan designed,
So cleverly it was built,
The whole proclaimed a master mind—
My Aunt Jemima's quilt.

Each friendly household far and wide
Contributed its share;
It chronicled the countryside
In colors quaint and rare.
From brides and grooms came rich brocade
Sewn through with threads of gilt;
Even clever cousins lent their aid
To Aunt Jemima's quilt.

No tapestry from days of yore,
No web from Orient loom,
But paled in beautiful tints before
This strange expanse of bloom.
Here glittering stars and comets shone
Over flowers that never wilt;
Here fluttered birds from worlds unknown
On Aunt Jemima's quilt.

Oh merry was the quilting bee,
When this great quilt was done;
The rafters rang with happy glee,
And hearts were lost and won.
Never did a throng of braver men
In war dash side by side,
Than sought the smiles of beauty then
Round Aunt Jemima's quilt.

This work of art my aunt esteemed
The glory of the age;
No poet's eyes have ever beamed
More proudly over his page.
Were other quilts to this compared,
Her nose would upward tilt;
Such impudence was seldom dared
Over Aunt Jemima's quilt.

Her dear old hands have gone to dust,
That once were lithe and light;
Her eager needles now coated with rust,
That flashed so nimbly bright.
And here it lies by her request,
Stained with the tears we spilt,
Folded safe in this cedar chest —
My Aunt Jemima's quilt.

FORMATIVE ASSESSMENT:
Main Idea

(1) What would be a good title for this story?

    A. Quilt of Beauty, Quilt of Pride

    B. Old Quilts are Collectable

    C. Quilting Bee Fun

    D. Quilting for Fun

(2) What was the main idea of the first stanza?

    A. Quilt making is a difficult hobby.

    B. Aunt Jemima's quilt was easy to construct.

    C. Aunt Jemima's quilt was extraordinarily beautiful.

    D. Aunt Jemima enjoyed sewing quilts.

(3) What is the main idea of the poem?

    A. how to have fun at a quilting bee

    B. the types of fabric used in quilts

    C. memories of an aunt and the beautiful quilt she made

    D. how to select bright colors and patterns for a quilt

(4) What is the main idea of the last stanza?

    A. Although Aunt Jemima is no longer alive, her quilt is still proudly protected by her family.

    B. Aunt Jemima is sadly missed.

    C. Aunt Jemima's sewing needles are rusty.

    D. Aunt Jemima's quilt is locked away because it is worth so much money.

FORMATIVE ASSESSMENT:
Supporting Details

1 Which detail from the poem does not support the beauty of the quilt?

   A. A miracle of gleaming dyes,

   B. So grandly was its plan designed,

   C. Oh never before by human eyes such gorgeous colors were seen!

   D. Each friendly household far and wide contributed its share;

2 Which detail from the last stanza helps show that the family still values Aunt Jemima's quilt?

   A. Her dear old hands have gone to dust,

   B. That once were lithe and light;

   C. Stained with the tears we spilt,

   D. Folded safe in this cedar chest-

3 Which detail from the poem helps show that the community supported Aunt Jemima's quilting?

   A. Her dear old hands have gone to dust,

   B. Her eager needles now coated with rust,

   C. Each friendly household far and wide contributed its share;

   D. It chronicled the countryside in colors quaint and rare.

4 Which detail from the poem does not help show Aunt Jemima's pride for her quilt?

   A. This work of art my aunt esteemed the glory of the age;

   B. No poet's eyes have ever beamed more proudly over his page.

   C. Were other quilts to this compared, her nose would upward tilt.

   D. The rafters rang with happy glee, and hearts were lost and won;

FORMATIVE ASSESSMENT:
Inferences

(1) How did Aunt Jemima feel her quilt compared to other quilts?

    A. She felt hers looked ugly compared to the other quilts.

    B. She felt her quilt and the other quilts were equally good.

    C. She felt her quilt was good, but others were better.

    D. She felt her quilt was much better than the other quilts.

(2) Where is Aunt Jemima's quilt at the end of the poem?

    A. somewhere in the countryside

    B. safe in a cedar chest

    C. covering Aunt Jemima's bed

    D. the poem does not reveal the location of the quilt

(3) How did Aunt Jemima's family feel about her quilt?

    A. The family valued it because it reminded them of Aunt Jemima.

    B. The family did not value it because it was old.

    C. The family had no strong feelings about the quilt.

    D. The family would give the quilt away if they could find someone willing to use it.

(4) The people in the community most likely reacted positively to Aunt Jemima's quilt because

    A. Aunt Jemima used beautiful colors and patterns in her quilt.

    B. Aunt Jemima was famous throughout the country.

    C. Aunt Jemima had known everyone in the community for many years.

    D. Aunt Jemima bought only the most expensive supplies for the quilt.

FORMATIVE ASSESSMENT:
Cause and Effect

(1) What caused Aunt Jemima's sewing needles to rust?

   A. The needles had not been used in a long time.

   B. Aunt Jemima's family members did not take care of the needles.

   C. The needles were an inferior quality.

   D. The needles were left in the rain.

(2) What caused Aunt Jemima's family to value the quilt?

   A. The quilt was valuable.

   B. The quilt was a work of art.

   C. The quilt reminded them of Aunt Jemima.

   D. The quilt was very old.

(3) Since the quilt was so beautiful the community felt

   A. awe.

   B. repulsion.

   C. disgust.

   D. contempt.

(4) The quilt was placed in a cedar chest because

   A. the family thought the quilt was too old to use.

   B. the family wanted to keep it safe.

   C. Aunt Jemima's son had requested it be place there.

   D. the family promised Aunt Jemima's husband they would keep it safe.

FORMATIVE ASSESSMENT:
Compare and Contrast

(1) How are Aunt Jemima and the people in the community alike?

   A. They believe her quilt is beautiful.

   B. They believe her quilt is simple.

   C. They believe her quilt could be better.

   D. They believe it took too long to complete the quilt.

(2) How are the first stanza of the poem and the last stanza of the poem different?

   A. The first stanza of the poem is light-hearted and merry, while the last stanza of the poem is dull.

   B. The first stanza of the poem is serious and sad, while the last stanza of the poem is light-hearted and merry.

   C. The first stanza of the poem is light-hearted and merry, while the last stanza of the poem is serious and sad.

   D. The first stanza of the poem is dull, while the last stanza of the poem is light-hearted and merry.

(3) According to the poem, Aunt Jemima's quilt is different than other quilts because Aunt Jemima's quilt

   A. was superior and the other quilts were inferior.

   B. was inferior and the other quilts were superior.

   C. took a long time to complete and other quilts were quickly completed.

   D. took a short time to complete and other quilts took a longer period of time to complete.

STORY SET 7

FORMATIVE ASSESSMENT:
Chronological Order

(1) Which event occurred AFTER Aunt Jemima's quilt was completed?

   A. She gathered material for the next quilt.

   B. She felt extremely proud of her quilt.

   C. She held a quilting bee.

   D. She planned the quilt's design.

(2) Which event did NOT occur BEFORE Aunt Jemima's needles began to rust?

   A. Aunt Jemima planned the quilt's design.

   B. Aunt Jemima's family packed the quilt away in a cedar chest.

   C. Friends contributed fabric for the quilt.

   D. A quilting bee was held.

(3) Place the events in chronological order.

   1. The quilt was placed in a cedar chest.

   2. A quilting bee was held.

   3. The design of the quilt was planned.

   4. The quilt became stained with tears.

   A. 1, 2, 3, 4

   B. 4, 3, 1, 2

   C. 3, 2, 4, 1

   D. 3, 1, 4, 2

FORMATIVE ASSESSMENT:
Author's Purpose and Perspective

(1) How does the author's tone change from the beginning of the poem to the end of the poem?

    A. It is cheerful in the beginning and thoughtful at the end.

    B. It is thoughtful in the beginning and cheerful at the end.

    C. It is sad in the beginning and friendly at the end.

    D. It is hostile in the beginning and serious at the end.

(2) How does the author view Aunt Jemima?

    A. with pride and tenderness

    B. with anger and disgust

    C. with warmth and hostility

    D. with pain and pity

(3) The author believes Aunt Jemima had a "master mind" for all of the following reasons except

    A. the plan for the quilt was grandly designed.

    B. beautiful colors were used in the quilt.

    C. Aunt Jemima had requested the quilt be stored in a chest.

    D. the quilt was cleverly made.

(4) Which word would the author agree describes Aunt Jemima?

    A. talented

    B. caring

    C. funny

    D. selfish

FORMATIVE ASSESSMENT:
Word Analysis

1 Read the following lines from the poem *Aunt Jemima's Quilt.*
Her eager needles now coated with rust,
That flashed so nimbly bright.
The word *nimbly* means

    A. quick and agile.

    B. slow and steady.

    C. sloppy.

    D. dimly.

2 Read the following line from the poem *Aunt Jemima's Quilt.*
Here fluttered birds from worlds unknown
The word *unknown* means

    A. not known.

    B. known again.

    C. relating to being known.

    D. usually known.

3 Read the following line from the poem *Aunt Jemima's Quilt.*
Each friendly household far and wide contributed its share;
The word *contributed* means

    A. gave.

    B. withheld.

    C. requested.

    D. took.

STORY SET 7

FORMATIVE ASSESSMENT:
Context Clues

1 Read the lines of poetry from *Aunt Jemima's Quilt*.
Were other quilts to this compared,
Her nose would upward tilt;
Such impudence was seldom dared
Over Aunt Jemima's quilt.
What does the word *impudence* mean?

   A. impoliteness

   B. kindness

   C. friendliness

   D. prejudice

2 Read the lines of poetry from *Aunt Jemima's Quilt*.
Her dear old hands have gone to dust,
That once were lithe and light;
What does the word *lithe* mean?

   A. elastic

   B. stiff

   C. rigid

   D. flexible and graceful

3 Read the lines of poetry from *Aunt Jemima's Quilt*.
No poet's eyes have ever beamed more proudly over his page.
What does the word *beamed* mean?

   A. clouded over

   B. to grimace in concentration

   C. to smile with joy

   D. to focus with intensity

FORMATIVE ASSESSMENT:
Synonyms and Antonyms

1 Read the line of poetry.
The rafters rang with happy glee
Which word is a SYNONYM for the word *glee*?

A. frenzy

B. calm

C. hopelessness

D. joy

2 Read the lines of poetry.
Never did a throng of braver men
In war dash side by side,
Which word is a SYNONYM for the word *throng*?

A. isolated

B. group

C. single

D. lone

3 Read the lines of poetry.
But paled in beautiful tints before
This strange expanse of bloom.
Which word is an ANTONYM for the word *strange*?

A. weird

B. odd

C. ordinary

D. possible

Young Benjamin Franklin

ADAPTED FROM A BIOGRAPHY BY NATHANIEL HAWTHORNE

Most people have heard of Benjamin Franklin, one of America's early leaders. However, most people have not heard the story of Benjamin when he was a young boy and the trouble he got into because he enjoyed fishing.

When Benjamin Franklin was a boy he was very fond of fishing. Much of his free time was spent catching flounders, perch, and eels.

The place where Benjamin and his friends did most of their fishing was a marshy spot on the outskirts of Boston. On the edge of the water there was a deep bed of mud. Benjamin and his friends were forced to stand in this mud while they caught their fish.

"This is very uncomfortable," said Benjamin one day to his friends as they were standing up to their knees in the quagmire.

"So it is," said Benjamin's friends. "What a pity we have no better place to stand!"

Not far from the mud bog, on dry land, there were many large stones that had been brought to be used in building a new house. Benjamin climbed onto the tallest stone.

Benjamin said, "I have a plan. It is awful to have to stand in the mud. See, I am filthy up to my knees, and so are all of you."

"I think we should build a dock to stand on while we are fishing. You see these stones?"

"The workmen are going to use them for building a house. I think we should take these stones, carry them to the edge of the water, and build a dock with them. What do you think? Should we build the dock?"

"Yes, yes!" cried the friends. "Let's do it!"

All the children agreed that they would meet there that night and begin building the dock by moonlight.

That night the children met and eagerly began to remove the stones. They worked like a colony of ants. Sometimes it would take two or three children to carry one stone. At last they had carried all of the stones away and built their little dock.

"Now," cried Ben, when the job was done, "let's give three cheers and go home to bed. Tomorrow we will catch fish."

"Hurrah! Hurrah! Hurray!" shouted his friends. Then they all scampered off and home to bed to dream of fishing.

In the morning, the workers came to begin building the house. They were very surprised to find all the stones gone! Looking carefully on the ground, the workers saw the tracks of many little feet, some with shoes and some without.

Following these tracks to the water, they soon found what had happened to the missing stones.

"Ah! I see what happened," one of the workers said. "Those little rascals who were here yesterday have stolen the stones to build a dock."

The worker was so angry he immediately went to the police and complained. The judge said Benjamin Franklin and the other children who were involved in stealing the stones should be punished.

Luckily, the owner of the stolen stones was forgiving. The gentleman respected Benjamin's father. He let the children go.

But the poor children still received punishment from their parents. Mr. and Mrs. Franklin were very disturbed by their son's actions.

"Benjamin, come here," said Mr. Franklin

The boy approached and stood in front of his father's chair. "Benjamin," said his father, "what could tempt you to take something that did not belong to you?"

"Father," said Benjamin, hanging his head at first, but then lifting his eyes to Mr. Franklin's face, "if it had been just for me, I would never have taken the stones. But I knew that the dock would help all the children with their fishing. If the owner of the stones built a house with them, then nobody would be helped except the owner of the house. I used them in a way that helped many children."

"My son," said Mr. Franklin, "evil can only produce evil and good can only come from good. It was evil to steal the stones. Only evil could come from it."

To the end of his life, Benjamin Franklin never forgot this conversation with his father.

FORMATIVE ASSESSMENT:
Main Idea

(1) What is the main idea of this passage?

   A. Benjamin Franklin improved the fishing area by providing a dock and in doing so became the hero of the town.

   B. Even though Benjamin Franklin meant well he still made a mistake.

   C. Benjamin Franklin enjoyed fishing and he would do whatever was necessary to improve the area in which he fished.

   D. Benjamin Franklin was an honest young man and when he borrowed the stones from the house the owner overreacted and called the police.

(2) What would be a good title for this story?

   A. Benjamin's Mistake

   B. Benjamin's Father Becomes Angry

   C. How to Build a Dock

   D. Benjamin and the Stones

(3) What is the main idea of the last paragraph of the story?

   A. Benjamin blamed his father for his mistake.

   B. Benjamin would always remember his mistake and not repeat it.

   C. Benjamin would soon forget his father's words.

   D. Benjamin disagreed with his father's words.

STORY SET 8

FORMATIVE ASSESSMENT:
Supporting Details

1 Which detail or quote from the story helps show that Benjamin Franklin regretted disappointing his father?

   A. To the end of his life, Benjamin Franklin never forgot this conversation with his father.

   B. The boy approached and stood in front of his father's chair.

   C. "Father," said Benjamin, hanging his head at first, but then lifting his eyes to Mr. Franklin's face, "if it had been just for me, I would never have taken the stones."

   D. "If the owner of the stones built a house with them, then nobody would be helped except the owner of the house."

2 How did the workmen know that children had stolen the stones?

   A. The workmen saw the children building the dock.

   B. The workmen saw the children's footprints.

   C. The workmen made the children admit their crime.

   D. Benjamin felt guilty and admitted he had taken all the stones.

3 Which detail from the story helps show that the workmen were angry with the children?

   A. The worker immediately went to the police and complained.

   B. The judge said Benjamin Franklin and the other children who were involved in stealing the stones should be punished.

   C. "Those little rascals who were here yesterday have stolen the stones to build a dock."

   D. The poor children still received punishment from their parents.

STORY SET 8

FORMATIVE ASSESSMENT:
Inferences

(1) What did Benjamin Franklin's father mean by the phrase "evil can only produce evil, good can only come from good"?

   A. Benjamin's father thought it was acceptable to do something wrong as long as it helped people.

   B. Benjamin's father thought if a wrong act was committed then the act could never help people.

   C. Mr. Franklin meant Benjamin should be able to do whatever he wanted to do.

   D. Benjamin's father meant it did not matter if someone committed a good or an evil deed.

(2) The reader can infer that

   A. the children were all in favor of building the dock.

   B. Mr. Franklin was in favor of building the dock.

   C. only a few children agreed the dock should be built.

   D. the other parents were not upset with their children helping to build the dock.

(3) Before Benjamin talked to his father he believed

   A. he was right to build the dock.

   B. he had made a mistake in building the dock.

   C. he should have put the stones back.

   D. he should have paid for the stones.

STORY SET 8

FORMATIVE ASSESSMENT:

Cause and Effect

(1) What caused Mr. Franklin to become upset with Benjamin?

   A. Benjamin built a dock.

   B. Benjamin influenced the other children and convinced them to build the dock.

   C. Benjamin went fishing without permission.

   D. Benjamin took something that did not belong to him without permission.

(2) What caused Benjamin to believe it was right to take the stones and use them in a dock?

   A. Benjamin believed if the stones were used for a dock it would help all the children.

   B. Benjamin thought the stones did not belong to anyone.

   C. Benjamin thought the owner of the stones would be understanding.

   D. Benjamin believed he could eventually pay the owner for the stones.

(3) Why did Benjamin want to build a dock?

   A. Benjamin thought it would be a challenge.

   B. Benjamin and his friends did not like standing in a quagmire.

   C. Benjamin and his friends were afraid poisonous snakes lived at the edge of the pond.

   D. Benjamin and his friends wanted to sneak out of their houses at night to build the dock.

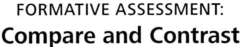

FORMATIVE ASSESSMENT:
Compare and Contrast

(1) How does Benjamin's feelings about the dock change from the beginning of the passage to the end of the passage?

   A. At the beginning Benjamin thought building the dock was the right thing to do, but at the end of the passage he felt it was wrong.

   B. Benjamin did not want to build the dock at the beginning of the passage, but at the end he was glad he had built the dock.

   C. Benjamin's feelings about the dock did not change from the beginning of the passage to the end of the passage.

   D. Benjamin only regretted he did not make the dock larger.

(2) According to the story, how were young Benjamin Franklin and his father different?

   A. Benjamin thought it was wrong to take the stones and his father thought it was acceptable.

   B. Benjamin thought it was acceptable to take the stones and his father thought it was wrong.

   C. Benjamin and his father thought it was acceptable to take the stones.

   D. Benjamin and his father both thought it was wrong to take the stones.

(3) According to the story, how were Benjamin and the other children different?

   A. Benjamin and the children all disliked standing in the quagmire.

   B. Benjamin wore shoes and the other children did not.

   C. Benjamin had the idea about building the dock and the other children only followed the plan.

   D. Benjamin followed the plan and the other children had the idea of building the dock.

FORMATIVE ASSESSMENT:
Chronological Order

1 Which event happened LAST in the story?

  A. Benjamin apologized to his father.

  B. Benjamin refused to listen to his father.

  C. Benjamin remembered what his father said.

  D. Benjamin thanked his father.

2 What happened immediately AFTER the workers arrived to begin building the house?

  A. The workers became angry.

  B. The workers discovered the stones were missing.

  C. The workers saw the footprints.

  D. The workers saw the dock.

3 At the beginning of the story, what were the children doing?

  A. moving stones

  B. building a dock

  C. fishing

  D. playing in the mud

4 What happened to the children AFTER the owner of the stones let them go?

  A. They tore down the dock.

  B. The apologized to the owner.

  C. They were punished by their parents.

  D. They were punished by the police.

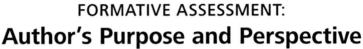

FORMATIVE ASSESSMENT:
Author's Purpose and Perspective

(1) Which word would the author agree best describes Benjamin Franklin?

    A. lazy

    B. entertaining

    C. quiet

    D. resourceful

(2) Which statement would the author probably agree with in regards to Benjamin's theft of the stones?

    A. Benjamin's father was disinterested.

    B. The owner of the stones was compassionate.

    C. The workmen were understanding about the theft of the stones.

    D. The children were resentful toward the workmen.

(3) How does the author probably feel about Benjamin Franklin at the end of the article?

    A. The author feels Benjamin learned a valuable lesson.

    B. The author feels Benjamin's punishment was too harsh.

    C. The author feels Benjamin will make the same mistake again.

    D. The author feels Benjamin did not like to listen to his father.

FORMATIVE ASSESSMENT:
Word Analysis

1 Read the sentence from the story.
The children worked like a colony of ants.
In the sentence the author means

    A. the children were playing.

    B. the children were working hard.

    C. the children were relaxing.

    D. the children were planning to fish.

2 Read the sentence from the story.
"This is very uncomfortable," said Benjamin one day to his friends, while they were standing up to their knees in the quagmire.
In the sentence the word *uncomfortable* means

    A. extremely comfortable.

    B. completely comfortable.

    C. sometimes comfortable.

    D. not comfortable.

3 Read the sentence from the story.
That night the children met and eagerly began to remove the stones.
In the sentence the word *eagerly* means

    A. enthusiastically.

    B. indifferently.

    C. halfheartedly.

    D. uninterestedly.

FORMATIVE ASSESSMENT:
Context Clues

(1) Read the excerpt.

"This is very uncomfortable," said Ben Franklin one day to his friends, while they were standing up to their knees in the quagmire.

What does the word *quagmire* mean?

A. snow

B. water

C. mud

D. grass

(2) Read this sentence from the story.

Then they all scampered off and home to bed to dream of fishing.

What does the word *scampered* mean?

A. ran quickly

B. stopped quickly

C. hid quickly

D. walked wildly

(3) Read the sentence from the story.

Those little rascals who were here yesterday have stolen the stones to build a dock.

As used in the sentence above, the word *rascals* means

A. evil people.

B. individuals who are mischievous.

C. angry children.

D. happy adults.

FORMATIVE ASSESSMENT:
Synonyms and Antonyms

(1) Read the sentence from the story.

But the poor children still received punishment from their parents.

Which word below is an ANTONYM for the word *punishment*?

A. reward

B. penalty

C. criticism

D. scolding

(2) Read the sentence from the story.

The worker was so angry he immediately went to the police and complained.

Which word below is the best SYNONYM for the word *immediately*?

A. soon

B. later

C. eventually

D. instantly

(3) Read the sentence from the story.

Mr. and Mrs. Franklin were very disturbed by their son's actions.

Which word below is the best SYNONYM for the word *disturbed*?

A. contented

B. satisfied

C. troubled

D. contented

The Man and the Nightingale

Once there was a very wealthy man. He lived in a large, beautiful house. The man had more gold than he could ever spend, all the delicious food he could eat, and hundreds of servants to do his bidding.

Yet the man was not happy. He always wanted more.

One night, the rich man lay in his bed thinking about all the new things he would buy the next day. Suddenly, the man heard the most beautiful song. It was the song of Nightingale, a little bird singing a song so beautiful it was like magic music sprinkled in the night air. Nightingale was singing happily in the man's garden.

The rich man lay listening to Nightingale's song throughout the long summer night. Nightingale sang the beautiful song over and over during the night. The man was so afraid he would miss Nightingale's beautiful song that he would not allow himself to go to sleep. As morning approached, the man's eyes were very heavy from lack of sleep. Just before his eyes closed he knew he must capture Nightingale so he could listen to its beautiful song whenever he wanted. The next night the rich, selfish man set a trap for Nightingale.

Sadly, Nightingale flew right into the man's trap.

"Now that I have caught you," the man cried, "you shall always sing to me."

But Nightingale had stopped singing. In fact, as soon as the door to the trap closed, Nightingale stopped singing.

"Sing! Sing!" cried the man.

"I never sing in a cage," said Nightingale unhappily.

The rich, selfish man was so angry he said, "Then I'll eat you. I have always heard that bird on toast is a tasty morsel."

"No! Do not kill me!" pleaded Nightingale. "Let me go free and I'll tell you three things worth far more than my poor body."

The man thought about this for a moment and then let Nightingale loose. Nightingale immediately flew up to a branch of a tree and said, "First, never believe a captive's promise. Second, do not sorrow over what is lost forever. My final piece of advice to you is to be happy with what you already have."

Then the songbird flew away and the rich man never saw him again.

STORY SET 9

FORMATIVE ASSESSMENT:
Main Idea

(1) What would be another good name for this story?

A. The Selfish Man and the Smart Bird

B. The Smart Man and the Selfish Bird

C. Nightingale's Big Day

D. How to Fool a Friend

(2) What is the theme of the story?

A. Possessions guarantee happiness.

B. Birds can provide happiness for only greedy people.

C. Greedy people can learn to share.

D. Greedy people remain greedy.

(3) What is the main idea of the second paragraph?

A. The rich man wanted to become even wealthier.

B. The rich man heard the song of a bird with a beautiful voice.

C. The bird wanted to leave the man's garden.

D. The man planned to capture the Nightingale.

FORMATIVE ASSESSMENT:
Supporting Details

(1) Which detail from the story helps show how beautiful Nightingale's voice sounded?

  A. The rich man lay listening to Nightingale's song throughout the long summer night.

  B. As morning approached, the man's eyes were very heavy from lack of sleep.

  C. The next night the rich, selfish man set a trap for Nightingale.

  D. Sadly, Nightingale flew right into the man's trap.

(2) What advice did Nightingale not give the rich man?

  A. Never believe a captive's promise.

  B. Do not sorrow over what is lost forever.

  C. Never sing in a cage.

  D. Be happy with what you already have.

(3) According to the story, which detail does not support the author's statement that the man was rich?

  A. The man lived in a large, beautiful house.

  B. The man thought about what he would buy the next day.

  C. The man had more gold than he could ever spend.

  D. The man captured Nightingale.

(4) What will the rich man do to Nightingale if the bird will not sing?

  A. He will free Nightingale.

  B. He will eat Nightingale.

  C. He will reward Nightingale.

  D. He will forgive Nightingale.

FORMATIVE ASSESSMENT:
Inferences

1) What lesson did Nightingale want the man to learn?

   A. Nightingale wanted the man to learn to be patient.

   B. Nightingale wanted the man to learn how to catch birds.

   C. Nightingale wanted the man to learn how to sleep when it's noisy.

   D. Nightingale wanted the man to learn to be happy with what he already had.

2) How did Nightingale know the rich man would release him from the cage if Nightingale promised the man three things that were valuable?

   A. Nightingale thought the man was stupid.

   B. Nightingale thought the man was evil.

   C. Nightingale thought the man could be easily tricked.

   D. Nightingale knew the man was greedy.

3) Why would the rich man rather eat Nightingale than set Nightingale free?

   A. The man thought if he could not enjoy Nightingale's singing, the man may as well enjoy the way Nightingale tasted.

   B. Nightingale was small enough to be a snack.

   C. Nightingale wanted to be a snack.

   D. The man thought if he could not enjoy eating Nightingale, the man may as well enjoy Nightingale's singing.

FORMATIVE ASSESSMENT:
Cause and Effect

1. Why was the rich man unhappy at the beginning of the story?

   A. The man always wanted more.

   B. Nightingale stopped singing.

   C. He was not able to go to sleep.

   D. He did not have enough gold to buy whatever he wanted.

2. Why did the rich man not allow himself to go to sleep the night he first heard Nightingale?

   A. The rich man was thinking of ways to catch Nightingale.

   B. Nightingale was making too much noise for the man to sleep.

   C. The man was thinking about everything he was going to buy.

   D. Nightingale's voice was so beautiful the man was afraid he would miss the singing if he went to sleep.

3. Why did the rich man trap Nightingale?

   A. to give Nightingale to his son

   B. to eat Nightingale on toast

   C. to move Nightingale out of the garden

   D. to keep Nightingale so he could hear the bird's beautiful song whenever he wanted

4. Why did the man let Nightingale go?

   A. He believed Nightingale would tell him something that would benefit him.

   B. He believed Nightingale would die if he did not let him go.

   C. He felt sorry for Nightingale.

   D. He decided he had been cruel to Nightingale.

FORMATIVE ASSESSMENT:
Compare and Contrast

(1) How are the characters of Nightingale and the rich man different from each other at the beginning of the story?

    A. The rich man is satisfied with life and Nightingale is not satisfied.

    B. Nightingale is satisfied with life and the man is not satisfied.

    C. Nightingale is quick to anger and the man is calm.

    D. The rich man is mad and Nightingale is happy.

(2) How are the characters of Nightingale and the rich man different from each other when Nightingale is trapped in the cage?

    A. Nightingale is happy and the rich man is sad.

    B. The rich man is happy and Nightingale is sad.

    C. The rich man is suspicious and Nightingale is trusting.

    D. Nightingale is suspicious and the man is trusting.

(3) How are the characters of Nightingale and the rich man similar?

    A. Neither enjoys Nightingale's singing.

    B. Both Nightingale and the man thought Nightingale sang too loudly.

    C. Both Nightingale and the rich man enjoy Nightingale's singing.

    D. Both Nightingale and the rich man enjoy singing.

(4) How did the character of Nightingale change?

    A. Nightingale did not change.

    B. Nightingale was afraid at the beginning of the story and brave at the end.

    C. Nightingale was careless at the beginning of the story and careful at the end of the story.

    D. Nightingale was careful at the beginning and end of the story.

FORMATIVE ASSESSMENT:
Chronological Order

(1) What happened just BEFORE Nightingale flew away?

  A. Nightingale sang one last song for the man.

  B. Nightingale told the man three things.

  C. Nightingale flew into the garden.

  D. The man let Nightingale out of the trap.

(2) What happened FIRST in the story?

  A. The man was in his bed thinking about what he was going to buy.

  B. Nightingale flew into the trap.

  C. Nightingale told the man three things.

  D. The man listened to Nightingale sing.

(3) What happened immediately AFTER Nightingale flew into the trap?

  A. Nightingale stopped singing.

  B. Nightingale flew away.

  C. The man made Nightingale sing.

  D. The man regretted the capture of Nightingale.

(4) What happened when the man heard Nightingale sing?

  A. He went to sleep.

  B. He built a trap.

  C. The man decided to let Nightingale go.

  D. The man stayed awake listening to Nightingale.

FORMATIVE ASSESSMENT:
Author's Purpose and Perspective

(1) What is the author's purpose in writing this story?

   A. to teach the reader how to catch a bird

   B. to entertain the reader with a story about a man and a bird

   C. to persuade the reader to go out and catch birds

   D. to explain why the rich man was unhappy

(2) With which statement would the author most likely agree?

   A. Nightingale made a mistake but was smart and thought of a way to get out trouble.

   B. The man realized he had made a mistake by capturing Nightingale.

   C. Nightingale was not smart enough to get out of the trap.

   D. The man was not smart enough to catch Nightingale.

(3) Which word below best describes the author's view about the rich man?

   A. ignorant

   B. generous

   C. smart

   D. selfish

(4) Nightingale can best be described as all of the following except being

   A. talented.

   B. intelligent.

   C. clever.

   D. greedy.

FORMATIVE ASSESSMENT:
Word Analysis

(1) Read this sentence from the story.

The next night the rich, selfish man set a trap for Nightingale.

What does the word *selfish* mean?

A. characterized by caring only for one's self

B. selfless

C. humane

D. not caring only for one's self

(2) Read this sentence from the story.

"I never sing in a cage," said Nightingale unhappily.

What does the word *unhappily* mean?

A. not happy or joyful

B. small happiness

C. greater happiness

D. in favor of happiness

(3) Read this sentence from the story.

Sadly, Nightingale flew right into the man's trap.

What does the word *sadly* mean?

A. to the extent of being sad

B. to the extent of being happy

C. to the extent of being glad

D. voluntarily sad

FORMATIVE ASSESSMENT:
Context Clues

(1) Read the sentence from the story.

Just before his eyes closed the man knew he must capture Nightingale so he could listen to its beautiful song whenever he wanted.

The word *capture* means to

A. trick.

B. lead.

C. remove.

D. trap.

(2) Read the sentence from the story.

The man had more gold than he could ever spend, all the delicious food he could eat, and hundreds of servants to do his bidding.

The word *bidding* means the servants will do as the man

A. commands.

B. asks.

C. pleads.

D. suggests.

(3) Read the sentence from the story.

It was the song of Nightingale, a little bird singing a song so beautiful it was like magic music sprinkled in the night air.

The word *sprinkled* means

A. enhanced.

B. dwindled.

C. declined.

D. scattered.

FORMATIVE ASSESSMENT:
Synonyms and Antonyms

(1) Which two words are ANTONYMS?

    A. captive/prisoner

    B. captive/detainee

    C. captive/free

    D. captive/hostage

(2) Which two words are SYNONYMS?

    A. trap/catch

    B. trap/free

    C. trap/release

    D. trap/liberate

(3) Which two words are SYNONYMS?

    A. delicious/tasteless

    B. delicious/tasty

    C. delicious/dull

    D. delicious/flavorless

(4) Which two words are ANTONYMS?

    A. approach/loom

    B. approach/retreat

    C. approach/proceed

    D. approach/advance

Polar Bears

White, soft, fluffy…these are words often used to describe polar bears. These beautiful bears live in the Northern Hemisphere on the Arctic ice cap. Polar bears spend most of their time in coastal areas due to seals being one of their primary food sources. Polar bears may travel long distances in search of food.

Polar bears and Alaskan Kodiak brown bears are the largest members of the bear family. These two types of bears are equal in size. Male polar bears are typically larger than the female polar bears. Male polar bears stand from 8 to 11 feet tall and generally weigh from 500 to 1,000 pounds. Some have weighed as much as 1,400 pounds. Female polar bears usually stand 8 feet tall and weigh 400 to 600 pounds, but may reach 700 pounds. Polar bears weigh so much because they store a lot of fat on their body. In order to stay warm, polar bears have about a 4-inch layer of fat on their body.

In addition to their large size, polar bears are different in other ways as well. Polar bears have longer, narrower heads than other bears. Polar bears' noses and ears are smaller than other bears.

Polar bears are different from other bears because of their coat color, too. Although the polar bear's coat appears white, each individual hair is actually a clear, hollow tube which tunnels the heat of the rays of the sun to the bear's skin and helps it stay warm. Some of the rays of the sun bounce off the fur, making the polar bear's coat appear white. During the summer months, adult bears shed their coats and grow new ones, which look pure white. By the following spring, the sunshine has caused their coats to turn a yellowish shade. Polar bears also sometimes have a yellowish shade to their coats caused by staining from seal oils.

The polar bear's coat helps it blend in with its snow-covered environment. The coat is a useful hunting adaptation. Fur covers the bottoms of its paws. This adaptation helps the polar bear keep from slipping on ice. Because the polar bear rarely eats plants, it is considered a carnivore, or meat-eater. The ringed seal is the polar bear's primary prey. A polar bear may hunt a seal by waiting quietly for it to come out from its blow hole, an opening seals make in the ice allowing them to breathe or climb out of the water to rest. The polar bear will often have to wait for hours for a seal to emerge. Because the polar bear's coat is white against the whiteness of the ice and snow, the seal may not see the hunting bear. Polar bears eat only the seal's skin and blubber, or fat, and the remaining left-over meat is an important food source for other animals of the Arctic. For example, Arctic foxes feed almost entirely on the remains of polar bear kills during the winter. The dead bodies of whales, seals, and walruses are also important food sources for polar bears. In fact, because of their sharp sense of smell, polar bears can sense dead animals from many miles away.

Polar bears can run very fast, but are most agile in the sea. They are excellent swimmers, and can reach speeds of up to 6 miles per hour in the water. They are good divers, too. When being pursued by hunters in open water, polar bears have been known to escape by plunging 10 to 15 feet below the surface and resurfacing a good distance away. They also have been seen swimming up to 100 miles away from ice or land.

A baby polar bear is called a cub. Usually two cubs are born in December or January. When the cubs first arrive, they are blind, hairless, and no bigger than squirrels. However, the cubs grow rapidly from the rich milk provided by their mother. As soon as spring comes, the mother bear leads her cubs to the coast along the open sea, where seals and walruses are plentiful. The mother will protect her cubs from any danger. The cubs remain with their mother for 2 1/2 years.

Polar bears have played an important role in the culture and livelihood of Eskimos and other Native people of the North. Eskimos and Native people depend on the animals for food and clothing. In the United States, polar bears are a federally protected species under the Marine Mammal Protection Act of 1972. This protection prohibits the hunting of polar bears. The Fish and Wildlife Service also undertakes education to inform the public about how polar bears can be protected. In Alaska, demands for oil, natural gas, and other resources have led to some conflicts between polar bears and humans. Protective measures have been taken to reduce the conflicts between man and the polar bears. Oil and gas pipelines and roads have been built to avoid polar bear areas.

	Polar Bear	Kodiak Bear
Body	• The polar bear is the largest member of the bear family, with the exception of the Kodiak brown bear. • Males can weigh as much as 1,400 pounds. • Males can be twice as large as females. • The polar bear's fur appears white.	• They are the largest bears in the world. • A male can weigh up to 1,500 pounds. • Males are larger than female Kodiak bears. • Kodiak bears have brown fur.
Habits	• Polar bears live only in the Northern Hemisphere on the Arctic ice cap. • Polar bears are carnivores, eating mostly meat. • The ringed seal is the polar bear's primary prey.	• Kodiak bears live on the islands in Kodiak Archipelago. • Kodiak bears are omnivores, eating plants and meat.
Life Span	• The oldest known polar bear lived for 33 years.	• The oldest Kodiak bear lived for 33 years.
Cubs	• Cubs are born in December or January. • They are blind and hairless at birth. • Polar bears usually give birth to two cubs. • Cubs stay with their mothers for approximately 2 years.	• Cubs are born during January or February. • Cubs have little hair at birth. • Cubs are born with their eyes closed. • Most mother Kodiak bears give birth to 2 or 3 cubs. • Cubs stay with their mothers for 3 to 5 years.
Government Protection	• Polar bears are a federally protected species under the Marine Mammal Protection Act of 1972.	• Kodiak National Wildlife Refuge was created in 1941. Stricter regulations enacted to protect the Kodiak went into effect at that time.

FORMATIVE ASSESSMENT:
Main Idea

(1) What is the main idea of the last paragraph from the passage?

   A. general information about polar bears

   B. the growth rate of polar bears

   C. polar bears and their adaptation to their environment

   D. protective measures that have been enacted to help protect the polar bear

(2) What would be a good title for this article?

   A. Interesting Facts About Polar Bears

   B. Amazing Kodiak Bears

   C. Polar Bear Cubs

   D. How Big Do Polar Bears Grow?

(3) This central point of the passage is

   A. to inform the reader about polar bears.

   B. to inform the reader about the diet of polar bears.

   C. to inform the reader about the size of polar bears.

   D. to compare polar bears and Kodiak bears.

FORMATIVE ASSESSMENT:
Supporting Details

1. How does the polar bear's sharp sense of smell help it survive?

    A. Polar bears can smell people from five miles away, thus always allowing the bears to escape.

    B. Polar bears can smell dead animals from miles away, thus allowing them to find meat to eat.

    C. Polar bears can smell oil and natural gas, thus allowing them to stay away from areas where people might work.

    D. Polar bears can smell plants from a great distance, thus allowing them to eat the plants when there is no meat available.

2. Why are polar bears important to Arctic foxes?

    A. Polar bears and Arctic foxes help each other hunt.

    B. Arctic foxes sleep in dens made by polar bears.

    C. Arctic foxes feed on food left by the polar bears.

    D. Polar bears keep other animals away from Arctic foxes.

3. Why do polar bears sometimes have a yellowish shade to their fur?

    A. Their fur becomes discolored by the sun.

    B. Their fur becomes yellow as the bears get older.

    C. Their fur becomes stained by dirt in the snow.

    D. Their fur becomes discolored by oil in the water.

FORMATIVE ASSESSMENT:
Inferences

(1) Why were oil and gas pipelines and roads built to avoid polar bear areas?

    A. to aid polar bears in finding food

    B. to protect polar bears from mankind

    C. to protect man from polar bears

    D. to aid polar bears in traveling on ice

(2) Why does the mother polar bear lead her cubs to the coast along the open sea in the spring?

    A. so the cubs can learn to swim

    B. so the cubs can enjoy the warmth of the spring sun

    C. so the cubs can be united with other polar bears

    D. so the cubs can find food

(3) The author might agree that polar bears

    A. are different than other bears.

    B. are often hunted.

    C. are the fastest animals on earth.

    D. are very similar to other bears.

(4) The reader can infer

    A. the author believes polar bears are interesting animals.

    B. the author believes polar bears will become extinct.

    C. the author believes polar bears are the most savage bears on earth.

    D. the author believes polar bears are more aggressive than the Kodiak bear.

FORMATIVE ASSESSMENT:
Cause and Effect

1. Why are polar bears important to Arctic foxes?

   A. Arctic foxes prey on the polar bears.

   B. Polar bears are not important to Arctic foxes.

   C. Polar bears build dens to share with the foxes.

   D. Arctic foxes eat the food that the polar bears leave behind.

2. According to the passage, why is the polar bear's sense of smell important for survival?

   A. The strong sense of smell allows the polar bear to find dead animals to eat.

   B. The strong sense of smell allows the polar bear to know when danger is near.

   C. The strong sense of smell allows polar bears to find other polar bears.

   D. The strong sense of smell allows polar bears to find the ocean from hundreds of miles away.

3. Why do polar bears weigh so much?

   A. Polar bears are muscular and muscle weighs more than fat.

   B. Polar bears are the largest mammals on earth.

   C. Polar bears have extremely heavy bones.

   D. Polar bears store a lot of fat on their bodies.

FORMATIVE ASSESSMENT:
Compare and Contrast

(1) How are polar bears and Kodiak bears alike?

   A. Polar bears and Kodiak bears both have white fur.

   B. Male polar bears and Kodiak bears are larger than the female bears.

   C. Polar bears and Kodiak bears both have long, narrow heads.

   D. Polar bears and Kodiak bears both mainly eat fish.

(2) Contrast the difference between polar bear cubs and Kodiak bear cubs.

   A. Polar bear cubs can see at birth, but Kodiak bear cubs are blind.

   B. Polar bears give birth to more cubs than do Kodiak bears.

   C. Kodiak bear cubs are born during the spring while polar bear cubs are born in the fall.

   D. Polar bear cubs stay with their mothers for a shorter period of time than do Kodiak bear cubs.

(3) How are polar bears and Kodiak bears different?

   A. Kodiak bears eat mostly meat and polar bears eat meat and plants.

   B. Polar bears live much longer than Kodiak bears.

   C. Kodiak bears are larger than polar bears.

   D. Polar bears have more cubs than Kodiak bears.

FORMATIVE ASSESSMENT:
Chronological Order

(1) According to the chart, which event occurred FIRST?

    A. The Marine Mammal Protection Act was created.

    B. Polar bears were placed on the endangered species list.

    C. Polar bears were relocated to the Arctic region.

    D. The Kodiak National Wildlife Refuge was created.

(2) What happens in the summer?

    A. Polar bears' coats turn yellowish due to staining.

    B. Polar bears shed their coats.

    C. Polar bears move to the coast.

    D. Polar bears give birth to several cubs.

(3) Which sentence tells what happens AFTER polar bear cubs are born?

    A. The cubs grow rapidly from the rich milk provided by their mother.

    B. Polar bears have played an important role in the culture and livelihood of Eskimos and other Native people of the North.

    C. When being pursued by hunters in open water, polar bears have been known to escape by plunging 10 to 15 feet below the surface and resurfacing a good distance away.

    D. A polar bear may hunt a seal by waiting quietly for it to come out from its blow hole, an opening seals make in the ice allowing them to breathe or climb out of the water to rest.

FORMATIVE ASSESSMENT:
Author's Purpose and Perspective

1 Why did the author write this article?

   A. to describe to the reader the appearance of polar bears

   B. to persuade the reader that polar bears should be protected

   C. to amuse the reader with facts about the polar bear's eating habits

   D. to inform the reader about polar bears

2 Why does the author include the chart on polar bears and Kodiak bears?

   A. to allow the reader to quickly compare facts about the two types of bears

   B. to allow the reader to place the facts in order

   C. to focus the reader on the most interesting facts about the Kodiak bear

   D. to provide information so the reader does not have to read the article

3 With which statement would the author of *Polar Bears* disagree?

   A. Polar bears are interesting animals.

   B. Polar bears have adapted to their environment.

   C. Polar bears' eating habits should be studied.

   D. All polar bears should be placed in zoos so they will remain safe.

4 The author of the article would best describe polar bears as all of the following except

   A. quick.

   B. large.

   C. camouflaged.

   D. silly.

FORMATIVE ASSESSMENT:
Word Analysis

① Read the sentence from the passage.

Because the polar bear's coat is white against the whiteness of the ice and snow, the seal may not see the hunting bear.

What does the word *whiteness* mean as used in the sentence?

A. one who is white

B. the state or condition of being white

C. product of being white

D. place for being white

② Read the sentence from the passage.

By the following spring, the sunshine has caused their coats to turn a yellowish shade.

What does the word *yellowish* mean as used in the sentence?

A. somewhat yellow

B. extremely yellow

C. opposite of yellow

D. not yellow at all

③ Read the sentence from the passage.

When being pursued by hunters in open water, polar bears have been known to escape by plunging 10 to 15 feet below the surface and resurfacing a good distance away.

What does the word *resurfacing* mean as used in the sentence?

A. to surface again

B. to surface often

C. to surface periodically

D. to not surface

FORMATIVE ASSESSMENT:
Context Clues

(1) Read this sentence from the article.

The polar bear will often have to wait for hours for a seal to emerge.

What does the word *emerge* mean?

A. draw into

B. come out

C. play

D. quickly swim

(2) Read this sentence from the article.

Polar bears can run very fast, but are most agile in the sea.

What does the word *agile* mean?

A. clumsy

B. alert

C. awkward

D. swift

(3) Read this sentence from the article.

When being pursued by hunters in open water, polar bears have been known to escape by plunging 10 to 15 feet below the surface and resurfacing a good distance away.

What does the word *plunging* mean?

A. diving

B. reducing

C. rising

D. striking

FORMATIVE ASSESSMENT:
Synonyms and Antonyms

1 Read this sentence from the article.

The coat is a useful hunting adaptation.

Which word is the best SYNONYM for the word *adaptation*?

A. edition

B. modification

C. version

D. fake

2 As used in the article, which is most SIMILAR to the word *narrower*?

A. thinner

B. wider

C. larger

D. lighter

3 As used in the article, which word is OPPOSITE to the word *hollow*?

A. empty

B. solid

C. sunken

D. worthless

4 As used in the article, which word is the best ANTONYM for the word *primary*?

A. main

B. chief

C. key

D. minor

ANSWER KEY

Story Set 1: Why the Ocean is Salty

Main Idea	1.B	2.A	3.A	
Supporting Details	1.D	2.C	3.B	4.A
Inferences	1.C	2.D	3.C	4.B
Cause and Effect	1.B	2.A	3.B	4.D
Compare and Contrast	1.C	2.C	3.D	
Chronological Order	1.D	2.B	3.B	
Author's Purpose and Perspective	1.B	2.A	3.B	4.B
Word Analysis	1.C	2.A	3.D	
Context Clues	1.A	2.C	3.A	
Synonyms and Antonyms	1.C	2.A	3.C	4.A

Story Set 2: The Blind Poet

Main Idea	1.A	2.A	3.A	4.D
Supporting Details	1.C	2.D	3.C	4.A
Inferences	1.B	2.D	3.D	4.A
Cause and Effect	1.C	2.C	3.C	4.D
Compare and Contrast	1.B	2.A	3.A	
Chronological Order	1.D	2.B	3.D	4.D
Author's Purpose and Perspective	1.A	2.C	3.B	4.B
Word Analysis	1.A	2.B	3.A	
Context Clues	1.B	2.D	3.C	
Synonyms and Antonyms	1.D	2.A	3.A	4.C

Story Set 3: Pandora and the Golden Box

Main Idea	1.B	2.B	3.A	4.A
Supporting Details	1.D	2.D	3.B	4.C
Inferences	1.D	2.D.	3.A	4.B
Cause and Effect	1.A	2.A	3.D	4.A
Compare and Contrast	1.A	2.D	3.B	
Chronological Order	1.C	2.B	3.D	4.B
Author's Purpose and Perspective	1.A	2.A	3.B	4.B
Word Analysis	1.A	2.D	3.C	
Context Clues	1.C	2.A	3.D	
Synonyms and Antonyms	1.A	2.B	3.A	

Story Set 4: The Oak Tree

Main Idea	1.C	2.A	3.B	4.B
Supporting Details	1.B	2.C	3.A	4.B
Inferences	1.A	2.B	3.A	4.A
Cause and Effect	1.D	2.B	3.A	4.A
Compare and Contrast	1.A	2.B	3.A	4.A
Chronological Order	1.A	2.D	3.B	4.A
Author's Purpose and Perspective	1.A	2.A	3.B	
Word Analysis	1.B	2.A	3.B	
Context Clues	1.A	2.B	3.A	
Synonyms and Antonyms	1.C	2.A	3.D	4.A

Story Set 5: Dinosaur National Monument

Main Idea	1.A	2.C	3.A	
Supporting Details	1.D	2.A	3.C	4.B
Inferences	1.A	2.B	3.C	
Cause and Effect	1.C.	2.A	3.B	
Compare and Contrast	1.B	2.A	3.A	
Chronological Order	1.B	2.A	3.D	
Author's Purpose and Perspective	1.B	2.B	3.A	
Word Analysis	1.C	2.B	3.D	
Context Clues	1.B	2.A	3.B	
Synonyms and Antonyms	1.D	2.C	3.A	

Story Set 6: Juan and His Painted Hat

Main Idea	1.A	2.B	3.D	
Supporting Details	1.D	2.A	3.C	4.A
Inferences	1.A	2.B	3.D	
Cause and Effect	1.B	2.D	3.B	
Compare and Contrast	1.B	2.A	3.A	
Chronological Order	1.C	2.C	3.B	
Author's Purpose and Perspective	1.B	2.C	3.D	
Word Analysis	1.A	2.D	3.D	
Context Clues	1.A	2.B	3.A	
Synonyms and Antonyms	1.B	2.D	3.C	4.C

Story Set 7: Aunt Jemima's Quilt

Main Idea	1.A 2.C 3.C 4.A
Supporting Details	1.D 2.D 3.C 4.D
Inferences	1.D 2.B 3.A 4.A
Cause and Effect	1.A 2.C 3.A 4.B
Compare and Contrast	1.A 2.C 3.A
Chronological Order	1.B 2.B 3.C
Author's Purpose and Perspective	1.A 2.A 3.C 4.A
Word Analysis	1.A 2.A 3.A
Context Clues	1.A 2.D 3.C
Synonyms and Antonyms	1.D 2.B 3.C

Story Set 8: Young Benjamin Franklin

Main Idea	1.B 2.A 3.B
Supporting Details	1.A 2.B 3.A
Inferences	1.B 2.A 3.A
Cause and Effect	1.D 2.A 3.B
Compare and Contrast	1.A 2.B 3.C
Chronological Order	1.C 2.B 3.C 4.C
Author's Purpose and Perspective	1.D 2.B 3.A
Word Analysis	1.B 2.D 3.A
Context Clues	1.C 2.A 3.B
Synonyms and Antonyms	1.A 2.D 3.C

Story Set 9: The Man and the Nightingale

Main Idea	1.A 2.D 3.B
Supporting Details	1.A 2.C 3.D 4.B
Inferences	1.D 2.D 3.A
Cause and Effect	1.A 2.D 3.D 4.A
Compare and Contrast	1.B 2.B 3.C 4.C
Chronological Order	1.B 2.A 3.A 4.D
Author's Purpose and Perspective	1.B 2.A 3.D 4.D
Word Analysis	1.A 2.A 3.A
Context Clues	1.D 2.A 3.D
Synonyms and Antonyms	1.C 2.A 3.B 4.B

Story Set 10: Polar Bears

Main Idea	1.D 2.A 3.A
Supporting Details	1.B 2.C 3.A
Inferences	1.B 2.D 3.A 4.A
Cause and Effect	1.D 2.A 3.D
Compare and Contrast	1.B 2.D 3.C
Chronological Order	1.D 2.B 3.A
Author's Purpose and Perspective	1.D 2.A 3.D 4.D
Word Analysis	1.B 2.A 3.A
Context Clues	1.B 2.D 3.A
Synonyms and Antonyms	1.B 2.A 3.B 4.D

CPSIA information can be obtained at www.ICGtesting.com
Printed in the USA
LVOW090400171212

311926LV00001B/1/P